Yosemite Valley
Bouldering

Yosemite Valley
Bouldering

by Matt Wilder

Published by
SuperTopo
2 Bradford Way
Mill Valley, CA 94941
www.supertopo.com

Written by Matt Wilder
Edited by Steve McNamara, Chris McNamara, Matt Wilder
Layout by Chris McNamara

Cover Photo: Lisa Rands climbing Thriller V10. *Photo by Wills Young*
Cover Horizontal Photo: El Capitan at Sunset. *Photo by Matt Wilder*
Back Cover Photo: Noah Kaufman on Atlantis V6. *Photo by Matt Wilder*
Opposite inside cover page: Josh Williams on Happily Ever After V6.
Photo by Matt Wilder
Contents photo: Lisa Davidson working a sloper on No Fur V3. *Photo
by Matt Wilder*

Wilder, Matt
Yosemite Valley Bouldering: SuperTopos

Contents

Warning!

Climbing and bouldering are inherently dangerous sports in which severe injuries or death may occur. Relying on the information in this book may increase the danger.

When climbing you can only rely on your skill, training, experience, and conditioning. **If you have any doubts as to your ability to safely climb any route in this guide, do not try it.**

This book is neither a professional climbing instructor nor a substitute for one. **It is not an instructional book. Do not use it as one.** It contains information that is nothing more than a compilation of opinions about bouldering in Yosemite Valley. **These opinions are neither facts nor promises.** Treat the information as opinions and nothing more. Do not substitute these opinions for your own common sense and experience.

Assumption of Risk

There may be errors in this book resulting from the mistake of the author and/or the people with whom they consulted. The information was gathered from a variety of sources, which may not have been independently verified. Those who provided the information may have made mistakes in their descriptions. The author may have made mistakes in their conveyance of the information in this book. **The author cannot, therefore, guarantee the correctness of any of the information contained in this book.** The topographical maps, photo-diagrams, difficulty ratings, danger ratings, protection ratings, approach and/or descent information, suggestions about equipment, and other matters may be incorrect or misleading. Fixed protection may be absent, unreliable, or misplaced. **You must keep in mind that the information in this book may be erroneous, so use your own judgement when choosing, approaching, climbing, or descending from a route described in this book.**

DO NOT USE THIS BOOK UNLESS YOU [AND YOUR ESTATE] PROMISE NEVER TO TRY TO SUE US IF YOU GET HURT OR KILLED.

Disclaimer of Warranties

THE AUTHOR AND PUBLISHER WARN THAT THIS BOOK CONTAINS ONLY THE AUTHOR'S OPINIONS ON THE SUBJECTS DISCUSSED. THEY MAKE NO OTHER WARRANTIES, EXPRESSED OR IMPLIED, OF MERCHANTABILITY, FITNESS FOR PURPOSE, OR OTHERWISE, AND IN ANY EVENT, THEIR LIABILITY FOR BREACH OF ANY WARRANTY OR CONTRACT WITH RESPECT TO THE CONTENT OF THIS BOOK IS LIMITED TO THE PURCHASE PRICE OF THE BOOK. THEY FURTHER LIMIT TO SUCH PURCHASE PRICE THEIR LIABILITY ON ACCOUNT OF ANY KIND OF NEGLIGENT BEHAVIOR WHATSOEVER ON THEIR PART WITH RESPECT TO THE CONTENTS OF THIS BOOK.

Acknowledgements

The following folks contributed beta, feedback, topos, photos, and support. Thank you!

Dan Wilder
Donna Wilder
Andrew Wilder
Randy Puro
Paul Barraza
Tim Medina
Courtney Hemphill
Lyn Verinsky
John Bachar
Tommy and Beth Caldwell
Dean Potter
Rick Cashner
Cedar Wright
Ivo Ninov
Noah Kaufman
Josh Williams
Brian Capps
Dean Fidelman
Wills Young
Matt Keebler
Jamie Emerson
Dave Pegg
Kay McNamara
Steve McNamara
Todd Offenbacher
Corey Rich
David Safanda
Randy Spurrier
Jonathan Thesenga

Preface

"Yosemite is a pile." "The bouldering is just a bunch of polished slabs and boring old-school mantels." "Camp 4 has more glassy surfaces than a skyscraper."

Why do I hear these kinds of comments so often? What's wrong with these people? Are they that out of touch with reality? Maybe they only bouldered in Yosemite on a 90-degree August day. Perhaps they didn't venture past the Wine Boulder, though they wouldn't have had to go far to find cool new problems. Or has this just become the accepted opinion about bouldering in Yosemite that people blindly perpetuate?

Snap out of it! Yosemite bouldering is amazing. I've bouldered in many of the world's best areas – Hueco Tanks, Fontainebleau, Grampians, The Buttermilks, Cresciano – and Yosemite is in the same league. The big beautiful boulders are covered with fun problems that require all different styles of climbing. And the potential for classic new problems is staggering. Sure the old school Camp 4 circuit is polished but that just means that you need to get out to the newer areas, or even go exploring and find completely new problems.

My first experiences with Yosemite bouldering ten years ago involved diligently working through the easier problems in the Camp 4. Soon however I became inspired to climb classics like King Cobra and Midnight Lightning. I would throw myself at these problems every chance I had, even during the lunch break from my janitorial job at the Degnan's pizzeria. After a few years of Valley bouldering, I began realizing that though Camp 4 certainly has its gems, many of the other areas offer a greater selection of fun moderates. In recent years I have been amazed by the potential for new problems and even whole new areas; it seems that I can't keep up with the rapid growth of my personal project list. While writing this book, I saw many climbed and unclimbed problems that I couldn't wait to try. I saw boulders with crazy features that had never been touched by climbers. Whole regions like the lower Merced Canyon (west of junction 140/120) and Mirror Lake have hardly seen any development.

I believe that now is the dawn of another bouldering revolution in Yosemite. If more of the bouldering energy that has been so rampant throughout the States in the past five years is directed toward Yosemite, stacks of modern classics will emerge. Highball aficionados will risk it on tall bold lines, compression kings will squeeze their way up nearly blank bulges, and crimp masters will find cool faces freckled with small edges. Alongside these desperates many fun moderates will also be established. It will take work and dedication but the results will be well worth the effort.

—Matt Wilder

Introduction

By Matt Wilder

When you come to Yosemite, there is no question about it, you're going to have a good time. There are a few things, however, that will make your trip more hassle free. In this section you will find lots of information that will make your visit even more enjoyable. However, for more updated and extensive information you should visit the Yosemite Beta Page on the SuperTopo web site: www.supertopo.com/climbingareas/yosemite.html

Getting There

Air Travel
The closest major international airports are Oakland International (3.5-hour drive) and San Francisco International (4-hour drive). Of the two, Oakland is preferred because it's less chaotic and 30 minutes closer to Yosemite. Sacramento International is also a 4-hour drive from Yosemite but has fewer connecting flights. Fresno Yosemite International is only a 3-hour drive but offers the fewest flights. Since all of these airports are about the same distance from Yosemite, shop around for the best fares. Some climbers fly into Los Angeles International, which is a 7-hour drive to Yosemite.

Train Travel
The train is not the fastest way to Yosemite but it's a cool way to travel. From Emeryville (a 20-minute bus ride from San Francisco) take Amtrak to Merced and board the Via Bus to Yosemite. There are three runs from Merced in the morning and one at 5:25 P.M. The cost is $20 round trip from Merced to Yosemite. From Los Angeles, Amtrak has a bus to Bakersfield that connects with a train to Merced. From there take the Via Bus to Yosemite.

Bus Travel
Short of having a car, the bus is the best way to get from a major airport to Yosemite. From Oakland, San Francisco, or Los Angeles take the Greyhound Bus to Merced and then the Via Bus to Yosemite. Plan a full day of travel if riding the bus. From June to November you can only reach Yosemite from Mammoth by the YARTS bus.

Car Travel
There are four state highways that access Yosemite: 120 from the west, 120 from the east, 140 from the west, and 41 from the southwest. The fastest access from the San Francisco Bay Area is 120. Highway 140 is the best option if coming from Los Angeles or Fresno. Highway 140 is also the lowest elevation road and offers the best winter access if 120 and 41 have chain controls (chains are rarely required on 140). Highway 120 from the east (aka The Tioga Pass Road) offers the best summertime access from Bishop, Utah, Nevada, and eastern states. However, this road closes after the first major winter storm (usually in November) and doesn't open until the snow melts (usually late May). To access Yosemite from the east in winter, you must get to the west side access roads by driving north through Tahoe or south through Bakersfield.

Rent a car at any airport or major city. International climbers who stay in the United States for more than a month often buy a used car in San Francisco or Los Angeles and sell it (or scrap it) at the end of their trip. To find a cheap car, look in the local papers or on www.craigslist.org.

Many people stay in Yosemite without a car. Renting a car is expensive and it's possible to reach most climbs by the free park shuttle bus.. Also keep in mind that gas is very expensive in the Valley—try to arrive with a full tank.

NOTE: Major changes are planned for Yosemite that will greatly affect transportation inside the Valley. Check the SuperTopo web site for the most current information on changing car restrictions and bus routes.

Randy Puro on The Shield V11, a problem he just put up. Photo by Matt Wilder.

Climbing

YOSEMITE
IS IT MADE OF LIMESTONE?

EL PORTAL
THE NEW SOHO?

HOT FLASHES:

SWAN SLAB GETS SLABBIER

CLIMBING BUM SPOTTED IN CAMP 4

BEARS REVOLT AGAINST RANGERS

CANNING – WHY IT'S HIP THIS SEASON

BLUE SUEDE SHOES TURNS BLACK

**PLUS: BANDANNAS, FIRÉS,
PAINTERS PANTS – FASHION EXPOSÉ**

SUBSCRIBE TODAY AT CLIMBING.COM

Driving times and distances to Yosemite Valley

From	Time (hours)	Distance (miles)
Boulder, CO*	20:00	1,254
Fresno, CA	2:20	90
Truckee, CA	4:00	240
Los Angeles, CA	6:00	311
Bishop, CA*	3:20	95
Oakland, CA	4:00	172
Sacramento, CA	4:00	174
Salt Lake City, UT*	12:00	707
San Francisco, CA	4:00	192
Tuolumne Meadows	1:30	60

*Driving times are 2 to 4 hours longer when Tioga Pass is closed, usually from November through May.

When to Climb

Spring and fall have the best climbing weather. Summer bouldering is usually uncomfortably hot. Winter can be perfect but can also have consecutive weeks of severe Sierra storms. A dry November is our favorite time in Yosemite—crisp temps and no crowds. For current road and weather conditions call 209-372-0200 AND check the many online forecasts.

Month	Average rainfall	Max/min temp in degrees F
January	6.35"	47/25
February	6.64"	55/26
March	5.87"	58/30
April	3.29"	65/34
May	1.48"	71/39
June	0.51"	80/46
July	0.29"	89/50
August	0.06"	89/50
September	0.55"	82/48
October	1.68"	72/39
November	3.49"	57/30
December	7.1"	49/26

Seasons

November–March The Valley empties of climbers and tourists. During this time there is usually an equal number of clear and stormy days. When bad weather rolls in, things get nasty very quickly. Pacific storms usually bring three days of heavy snow or rain but can last up to a week or longer. Most boulders dry fast but a few can take days or weeks to dry out. If a two-week storm system rolls in, it's time to ski or snowboard at Badger Pass in Yosemite or head to Joshua Tree. If camping in the Valley during the winter, prepare for long cold nights.

April–May 15 The Valley is still uncrowded. It's warmer, but there is the same 50/50 chance of getting either good or miserable weather. If you are traveling from far away this is a risky time to visit, especially if you only have a week or less of vacation.

May 15–June Warm weather and big crowds of both tourists and climbers. Temps will start to get too warm for the hard projects. At some point in June the mosquitos show up and can be nasty.

July–August The Valley is still crowded with tourists, but most climbers head to Tahoe or Tuolumne for cooler weather. Valley floor temperatures are often in the 90s and 100s.

September–October The Valley is crowded with tourists and climbers. The weather usually begins warm and then cools sometime in October. Most days in October are great for bouldering. The first winter storm usually arrives in late October or early November.

Staying in the Park

Yosemite Valley is a small tourist town filled with buildings, roads, cars, and people. The bad news is that the restaurants, stores, and motel-like rooms take away from the natural beauty of the park. The good news is that these same things make the Valley

THE MOST ADVANCED BOULDERING SYSTEM EVER

WE DON'T MAKE MATS - WE ENGINEER THEM

UP TO 40% MORE ENERGY ABSORPTION THAN OPEN CELL FOAM

MORE DURABLE THAN OPEN CELL FOAM

MORE COMPACTABLE THAN OPEN CELL FOAM

FOR DETAILED INFORMATION OF OUR PRODUCTS
WWW.FLASHED.COM

DISTRIBUTED IN THE US BY GREAT TRANGO HOLDINGS INC.
WWW.FLASHEDUSA.COM

move with confidence

A slackline properly rigged in Camp 4.

quite accommodating. You will find pizza, burgers, groceries, climbing gear, a medical clinic, motels, swimming pools, rafts, bike rentals, and if you're unlucky, The Hotel John Muir (jail).

Camping

Camp 4 is the historic center of American climbing. It is also Yosemite's only walk-in campground and the cheapest place to stay. No reservations are required, but during peak season (May–October) expect a long wait to secure a campsite. The cost is $5 per person per night. Each six-person site is a 20-foot-square patch of dirt with fire pit and picnic table. If there are fewer than six people in your group you will share the site with others. There is a bathroom and a sink in the middle of Camp 4, but no hot water or showers. A bulletin board next to the Ranger Kiosk offers the chance to find climbing partners, friends, and used climbing gear. All other Yosemite campgrounds require reservations during peak season. Call 800-436-PARK to make reservations or go online to: http://reservations.nps.gov

There are a variety of places to camp outside the park boundary on Forest Service Land. Check out the Forest Service web site for more info: www.r5.fs.fed.us

Lodges and Cabins

For the big bucks, you can stay at the Ahwahnee Hotel, or for a more modest price you can crash in a motel-like room at the Yosemite Lodge or a canvas-topped cabin in Curry Village. Also, vacation homes are located just minutes out of the Valley in Foresta (with views of the summit of El Capitan and Half Dome). Check out the awesome cabins at www.4yosemite.com or call 800-723-4112 and ask about the climbers' specials. In the summertime your best bet is to make reservations well in advance of your visit. Spaces fill up early for lodges and cabins in the tourist season of June–September.

nicros
Simply The Best
check out all of nicros shapes
the strongest and lightest holds ever made
we make climbers and handholds stronger™
800.699.1975
www.nicros.com

Food

Groceries are available in the Valley at the Village Store, Curry Village Store, or Lodge Store, but it is much cheaper to buy groceries in Oakdale, Merced, or Oakhurst on the drive to Yosemite.

There are a variety of restaurants in the Valley that serve everything from pizza and deli sandwiches to the spendy stuff at the Ahwahnee Hotel. Here is a quick listing of some of the Valley restaurants by location:

Yosemite Lodge: "The Caff" (cafeteria), Mountain Room Bar and Grill.

Yosemite Village: Degnan's Deli, The Loft (pizza and pasta), burger stand.

Curry Village: Pizza Deck (with bar), buffet, taco shop.

Showers and Laundry

Showers cost $3 (towel included) and are available at Housekeeping or Curry Village. Laundry is available at Housekeeping.

Climbing Gear and Climbing Guides

The Mountain Shop (209-372-8396), located in Curry Village, is one of the premiere climbing shops in The West. From bouldering pads to haulbags to the latest route beta, they have it all.

Need a stick brush?

You can get climbing instruction, arrange for a guide, and also rent gear from the Yosemite Mountaineering School and Guide Service. There are also a variety of climbing shops in the San Francisco Bay Area where you can purchase gear. In San Francisco: Mission Cliffs and The North Face. In Berkeley: REI, Wilderness Exchange, Berkeley Ironworks, and Marmot Mountain Works.

If you are coming from the east side of the Sierra, then visit Wilson's Eastside Sports in Bishop or Mammoth Mountaineering Supply in Mammoth—both have an extensive selection of rock climbing and mountaineering gear.

Bears

Bears have damaged cars for as little as a stick of gum or an empty soda can. If you want what's yours to remain yours, remember three things: bears are hungry, smart, and strong. Bears are responsible for close to a thousand car break-ins every year in Yosemite, as all the shattered glass in the parking lots will tell you.

When bears smell food, even if it's locked in your trunk or glove compartment, they shift into high gear. They get turned on by odors of containers that used to contain food, and for toothpaste and sunscreen. Bears don't even need to smell food; they see something like a grocery bag or an ice chest, and associate it with food. In fact, they don't need to see that much. If a bear notices clutter inside a car, he'll think, "I wonder what's under all that stuff?" and go to work.

Breaking into a car is a trivial exercise for a bear. He inserts his claws at the top of the door frame and pulls down. Then he climbs in and trashes the car. You can't outsmart or out-muscle a bear. Stash your food in one of the bear-proof storage lockers provided by the Park Service at all campgrounds and throughout the Valley. Proper food storage is essential to protecting your property and more importantly the life of the bear. When a bear starts to endanger people it may be killed by the Park Service. Visit www.nps.gov/yose/bears.htm for more info.

Sometimes we get so excited about why we came that we forget to stop and look around … to appreciate the infinite mystery overhead or the possibilities right in front of us. That's why we make comfort and ease-of-use top priority in our shelters, whether for surfing expeditions or for NASA missions. That way you have a little extra time to take a deep breath and remember where you are.

We build extraordinary shelters for earthly exploration and beyond. Adventure Anywhere™

Moonshine meditation.

NEMO founder Cam Brensinger wakes up to catch the first waves with NEMO designer Ahern Laurinat on a frigid November morning near their shop in New Hampshire.

www.nemoquipment.com 603.881.9353

NEMO

Setting sun over the Cathedrals.

Poison Oak

Poison Oak grows sporadically throughout the Valley, especially in the Lower Merced Canyon west of the 120/140 junction. Find someone to show you what it looks like and be especially careful in the winter when poison oak loses its leaves and is difficult to see.

Internet

Though you should be eschewing computers while on vacation in the Valley, there are a few places where you can take care of internet needs. The only place for free internet is the Library / Girls Club which is near the visitor center in Yosemite Village. There time is limited and long waits are expected. The Yosemite Lodge offers two alternatives. In the Lodge lobby there are several terminals where you can access the internet for the exorbitant rate of $0.25 per minute. The Lodge also has wireless access that can be purchased for a flat daily rate – inquire at the front desk.

Rules To Keep in Mind

Yosemite is a great place to stay but if you don't know the some important park rules, a shadow can be cast over your trip. Here are a few park rules that are useful to know:

• Each person can stay a maximum of seven days between April 30 and September 30 and a total of 14 days throughout the whole year. The rangers keep track of your name in Camp 4 and require an ID when you register.
• Camping out of bounds in illegal and is subject to a fine around $100. Camping at the base of cliffs is considered out of bounds.
• Parking in Camp 4 without a pass is not permitted. The rangers often check this lot and the fine can be quite pricey (around $95). The same applies to the Yosemite Lodge parking lot and other lots that are not designated as day-use.
• Do not leave food in your vehicle; you will be fined. If a bear breaks into your car, you will still be fined and you will have to fix your car.
• Yosemite is federal land and so all federal laws apply.
• Slacklines can only be set up inside Camp 4; lines set up elsewhere will be confiscated. All trees must be adequately padded to avoid damage. (See photo on page 15.)
• Bear boxes in Camp 4 are only for registered campers. The rangers will

occasionally confiscate food from bear lockers if they think it belongs to someone not staying in the site.

• Rangers regularly stop cars for speeding; obey the speed limits throughout the park.

• Any gear left unattended for more than 24 hours can be confiscated.

• Open container laws apply in the Valley. You can only drink alcohol in your campsite, at an establishment that serves alcohol, or someone's residence.

Bouldering Etiquette

There are not typically many rules associated with bouldering, however there are a few that are important to follow while bouldering in Yosemite Valley. By not adhering to these ethics, you are taking away from the experiences of other climbers and damaging the climber-park relationship. These are the major rules to follow but not all of them; please use your common sense when it comes to what is appropriate behavior.

Chipping of any problems or holds is strictly prohibited, regardless of whether the problem is old or new. When you chip a problem, you are making a permanent change to it that lowers its difficulty to your level. This undignified act limits all future enjoyment of the problem. Chipping has not been a significant problem in Yosemite—let's keep it this way.

There are occasionally loose flakes on the Yosemite boulders and it can be tempting to consider gluing a hold to make a problem go. Gluing holds, however, is unacceptable and should not be done. If a hold is too loose to hold body weight, then it shouldn't be part of the problem. If the problem can't be done without the use of a hold that will break, then the problem shouldn't be done. There are plenty of great problems in Yosemite, there is no need to create another one with a mess of glue.

Pof or rosin should not be used in Yosemite. It leaves a permanent residue on problems that creates a glassy texture. Hand drying agents that contain rosin are not permitted, nor is colored chalk.

Beta and tick marks have become a core component of bouldering culture. However, it's important to realize that not all boulderers want beta for a problem or tick marks on it. Before shouting beta to the girl you just met, first ask her if she wants it. When using tick marks, be discreet (i.e. no long arrows and circles) and remember to remove them with a brush when you leave the problem.

Wire brushes should not be used in Yosemite on any established problems.

When attempting problems be sure to respect the nearby vegetation. Don't place pads on top of plants and avoid stepping on any natural life when spotting. If a problem can only be climbed by breaking these rules, don't try it.

Finally, please be sure to not leave any trash in the boulders. Most importantly, this includes athletic tape scraps. In the past years this has become more of a problem. It's not that hard; when you take tape off your fingers, put it in your pocket or in your bag, not on the ground where it's easy to forget.

First Ascents

Yosemite's bouldering potential is untapped and everyone is encouraged to explore the Valley and develop new problems. In addition to the general bouldering rules, there are a few other things to keep in mind when putting up a new problem. Generally, the goal is to minimize impact. The main issue in Yosemite involves brushing off moss. If a boulder is covered in moss, it is probably best to leave it that way. When removing moss, definitely don't just brush circles around the holds or a streak up the boulder. Make an effort to leave the moss in natural shapes. When doing a first ascent, remember that you want to problem to be aesthetically pleasing to the people that climb it after you. Report first ascents to www.supertopo.com – include the name, grade, description, and location.

Uncompromising
products
for the
well-rounded
–Always between you and the ground
www.bluewaterropes.com
770-834-7515

Bouldering History

By Matt Wilder

(References: "Camp 4: Recollections of a Yosemite Rockclimber" by Steve Roper, "Stone Crusade: A Historical Guide to Bouldering in America" by John Sherman, "A History of Free Climbing in America" by Pat Ament, "Yosemite: Half a Century of Dynamic Rock Climbing" by Alexander Huber and Heinz Zak)

Of all climbing areas in the states, Yosemite probably has the richest climbing history. Though the focus of climbing there has been the taller cliffs, a significant amount of time has been devoted to ascending the little stones. Bouldering began in the 1940s but was generally regarded as practice climbing. A few Valley locals used the Camp 4 boulders to hone their rock technique. The only significant problem from this period is the Steck Overhang (5.10+) on the Big Columbia Boulder, presumably done first by Allen Steck in the late 40s or early 50s. During this time period, climbers ascended the bigger cliffs using aid and free – the specific type of climbing was not greatly emphasized. With no specific importance placed on free climbing, bouldering as a sport of its own did not yet make sense.

In 1953, when Royal Robbins began his sojourn in the Valley, the only Valley test piece was the Steck Overhang. This was soon to change though as climbing grew in popularity and a greater emphasis was placed on free climbing. Robbins, a major player in the Yosemite climbing and bouldering scene of the 1950s and 60s, was known for his great technique and footwork on the boulders. Robbins repeated the Steck Overhang and soon began adding his own problems to the Camp 4 circuit, which at the time included only the Columbia Boulders, the Wine Boulder, and a few boulders surrounding the Wine Boulder. One of Robbins' new problems was The Robbins Pull Up (a.k.a. The Robbins Eliminate) which was likely V1 – holds on this problem have been exfoliated by campfires and the problem no longer exists.

Another interesting legend from this time period involves the naming of the Wine Boulder. The story depicts a typical Camp 4 scene in the mid to late 50s with several climbers hanging out drinking wine. Warren Harding, no stranger to the wine jug, claimed to be able to climb the Wine Boulder with a glass of wine in hand. Naturally some people believed his claim while others remained skeptical. These two groups undoubtedly argued for a while until they realized that the only way to reach resolution was for Harding to directly prove his claim. So the crew marched up to the boulder and Harding dispatched the Wine Traverse with glass of wine in hand. In other versions of this legend, Bob Swift is the wine-bearing climber.

Bouldering development during the 50s was still very slow and did not extend beyond Camp 4. In 1958 Chuck Pratt joined the Yosemite scene. Though not particularly inspired by bouldering, Pratt was known as a manteling expert. Pratt was, however, dedicated to free climbing and completed the first free ascents of many cracks throughout Yosemite. By the early 60s, Pratt was the best free climber in the Valley. In one story that demonstrates his impressive ability, Pratt left the campfire at night after having a few drinks and climbed the slabby west face of the Big Columbia boulder in his clunky boots without using the chipped holds. Anyone who has climbed this route knows that the problem is not over when you reach the slabbier rock ten feet off the deck. Here there are still a few tricky slab moves that are hard even with sticky rubber. In the dark with clunky boots, these moves must have been terrifying, but Pratt mastered the situation.

Layton Kor and Bob Kamps were two other climbers that contributed to Yosemite bouldering during the early and mid 60s. Kor's most significant addition is probably the Kor Problem, a classic 5.11 (V3) technical face.

As free climbing gained popularity on the big cliffs, bouldering began to gain a more meaningful purpose. Bouldering was still primarily thought of as training, but climbers started heading to the boulders more and more. In 1965 Jim Bridwell arrived in Camp 4 and was soon to take his seat in the Yosemite free climbing throne. Bridwell focused predominantly on roped climbing, but left a few marks on the bouldering history and a Swan Slab boulder bears his name.

In the late 60s, bouldering in Yosemite finally became recognized by some as an end in itself. Pat Ament, one of the first climbers that preferred bouldering, was a significant figure during this period. In the spring of 1968, Ament introduced gymnastic chalk to the Valley. Since the Camp 4 granite was more or less as slick then as it is now, the arrival of chalk must have been appreciated by most. In this same year, Ament did the first ascent of the Ament Arête (B1+, V5). Though it's likely that the difficult sit start to this problem was added later, even the stand start to this problem requires significant power and technique – from a slopey jug you reach with your left hand to a small sidepull crimp, then you make a long move to the lip of the boulder. The gymnastic movements of the slightly overhanging Ament Arête foreshadowed a new type of bouldering that was possible on the beautiful granite blocks of Yosemite

Nevertheless, manteling and slab climbing remained the most popular style of climbing from the late 40s until the mid 70s. One of the most famous Yosemite mantels ironically is not on a boulder. In the Yosemite Lodge, one of the rooms was designated as the guest lounge. Because this lounge was not frequented by the management, it proved to be a good place for climbers to hang out. In the middle of the room was a fireplace with a large angled metal hood that caught the smoke. As it turns out, the angle of the hood was just right to make for a possible but very difficult mantel. The difficulty was compounded by the fact that the hood hung freely, which meant there was no place for the manteler's legs and feet. It's not clear who did the first ascent of this mantel, but the problem remained a formidable test piece for years – you couldn't call yourself a Yosemite climber unless you had done this mantel. This fireplace still exists, though it is conspicuously located in the middle of the Mountain Room Bar.

By the early 70s another climber, Barry Bates, had risen to the top of the Yosemite bouldering community. Bates spent significant time bouldering and was known for his legendary strength – he could do one finger pull-ups and had a daily routine which included five sets of 20 fingertip pull-ups. Bates is credited for the first ascent of the Bates Problem (B1, V4). Though not the very hardest problem when it was established, the Bates Problem was significant because it climbed the steep, seemingly blank north side of the Big Columbia boulder. The climb starts with tricky undercling moves and progresses to a series of wide, powerful gaston crimp moves. Several delicate foot placements are required before you reach the big jug 13 feet off the deck. The climbing from the jug to the summit is easier but still heady. The Bates Problem represents a shift towards what is now considered modern bouldering; it follows a straight line up a tall aesthetic face and requires a synthesis of power and technique. Though Bates regularly climbed the Bates Problem, he thinks that it may have actually been done first by Steve Wunsch. Bates, with his dedicated training practices, also served as a source of inspiration for the upcoming generation of climbers.

The early 70s was also the beginning of a new era of climbing footwear. EBs, with their flexible rubber soles, replaced the rope-soled kletterschuhe as the preferred climbing shoe. This advancement in footwear undoubtedly helped climbers push the standards and made problems like the Bates Problem and Blue Suede Shoes easier. EBs gave climbers more sensitivity and allowed them to mold their feet to the contours of the rock. They did not however have the sticky rubber that modern climbing shoes now have.

By the mid 70s a new breed of climber was forming in the Valley. The stonemasters had arrived and were quickly building on the accomplishments of the previous generation. Climbers like John Long, Dale Bard, Mike Graham, Tobin Sorenson, John Bachar, John Yablonski, Lynn Hill, Mark Chapman, Ron Kauk, and Rick Cashner greatly advanced the level of free climbing on the walls and boulders. Even though the stonemasters still focused on roped climbing, they accepted bouldering as end in itself. This was the first time in Yosemite history that more than one or two climbers showed serious dedication to bouldering. This increased interest resulted in the development of many new problems, including some all-time classics.

The most significant first ascent, perhaps in the history of bouldering throughout the world, was completed in 1978. At this point there were several problems on the Big Columbia boulder in the middle of Camp 4 and it seemed that there were no more climbable faces. In the midst of an acid trip, unhindered by dogmatic beliefs about what is possible, John "Yabo" Yablonski envisioned a ludicrous line up the center of the northeast face. Yabo showed the line to the top boulderers of the time, Ron Kauk and John Bachar. Both climbers were skeptical of the line's feasibility at first but decided to attempt it nonetheless. After several weeks of slowly unlocking the now iconic intro moves, the two were able to get to the lip and found themselves trying to solve the challenging mantel. Each climber took

numerous falls onto the unforgiving granite slab 12 feet below the lip. Finally, after days of work, Kauk pushed himself a little bit farther into the mantel and just managed to reach the better holds above—Midnight Lightning was born. Shortly after Kauk's send, Bachar broke the thumb-shaped edge at the lip that seemed necessary for the mantel. Kauk, was outraged thinking that the problem was now impossible. Bachar, however, was still inspired to climb this amazing line. Eventually he repeated the problem via an even more tenuous mantel. Bachar then wired Midnight Lightning so completely that he could repeat it many times in a day and could climb it barefoot. At the time, Bachar and Kauk were using a modified version of the YDS scale to rate boulder problems – Midnight Lightning was given 5.12c. When the Font scale came to Yosemite, the problem was rated 7b+. Now Midnight Lightning is thought to be the standard for V8, if not a bit on the hard side.

Midnight Lightning is an important milestone in American bouldering. It represents a significant advancement in difficulty as well as a shift in climbing style. The problem requires a balancy yet powerful undercling move, a precise deadpoint, a finger-strength-intensive match, and a super technical mantel that can't be done without the correct body position. It ascends the middle of a tall beautiful face and relies heavily on the macro features that the rock presents. Boulderers continue to seek these same characteristic in the boulder problems they climb today. Midnight Lightning showed climbers how majestic the bouldering experience can be – the days of short slabs and single move mantels were in the past.

For a while after the first ascent of Midnight Lightning, many new problems were done in the same difficulty range, but nothing harder was climbed. One such problem was another desperate mantel, Purple Barrel, ascended by Bachar and named after a particularly popular type of acid. In 1984 Kauk again raised the difficulty bar in Yosemite and America with Thriller. On

Kauk's and Bachar's YDS bouldering scale, the problem weighed in at 5.12d, though it was significantly harder than Midnight Lightning. Now thought of as solid V10, Thriller was one of the hardest boulders in the country when Kauk did the first ascent. Thriller was significant for its beauty, not just its pure difficulty. Located in a beautiful setting in the corner of Camp 4, Thriller climbs the center of an amazing, slightly overhanging wall that is 40 feet wide and 18 feet tall. The holds on the route are perfect and the movement is intricate and intriguing.

Around the same time as the first ascent of Thriller, Bachar imported sticky rubber to Yosemite. For a while Miguel Angel Gallego from Spain was going around Camp 4 touting his new shoes. Finally giving in to Gallego's entreaties, Bachar threw on a pair slightly too big for him and marched up to Blue Suede Shoes. Despite the bagginess of the shoes, Bachar waltzed up the problem, quickly realizing the impact these new shoes would have on climbing. The shoes were called Fires (pronounced Fee-rays) and were similar to EBs except for the fact that the friction with the rock was much better. In 1985, shortly after the Fires arrived, America's first sticky rubber, Stealth, was developed and affixed to climbing shoes. Since the development of sticky rubber, climbing shoes have not improved much, though rubber has become slightly stickier and different shapes have been designed that increase toe power and improve performance for specific styles of climbing.

Throughout the rest of the 80s there was a lull in Yosemite climbing and bouldering that primarily resulted from the increased popularity of sport climbing. Though the standards weren't raised during this time period, Valley locals continued developing problems throughout the Valley. It was during this period that climbers began really exploring the bouldering potential outside of Camp 4.

In the early 90s, Jerry Moffatt visited the Valley and was enchanted by the beautiful boulders. In 1992, after repeating many of Kauk's test pieces, Moffatt set his sights on some unclimbed faces. First he dispatched Stick It (8a, V11), a slopey lip and face on the trail side of the Wine Boulder. He also scoped a line left of Thriller, but felt that the landing needed some work. With Kauk's help, Moffat dug up part of the landing, placed pallets underneath the problem, and then covered the pallets. Shortly after climbing Stick It, Moffatt was feeling particularly light and surprised himself by climbing through the lower part of the problem left of Thriller. He was close to the top but still needed to make a move from a sloper to a good hold far to the left. Surprising himself again, he stuck the hold out left and then encountered a dirty topout – he hadn't cleaned the top yet because he wasn't expecting to get there. Moffatt pulled through the mossy holds completing the first ascent of The Force (8a, V11). The problem has changed since the first ascent and is now considerably easier (see the problem description). Before leaving the Valley for the season, Moffatt eyed the steep face right of his new problem Stick It – this project was worthy of a future trip to Yosemite.

Sure enough, Moffatt returned in 1993 to attempt the steep face on the Wine Boulder. Moffatt found a sequence for the second part of the problem, but was stymied by the first move, which required a difficult swing after a long deadpoint from a slopey block to a small slopey edge. The move was desperate; there was practically nothing for Moffatt to use to stay on at the apex of the swing. Moffatt took a rest day during which he hiked extensively and ate minimally. Early the next morning, he returned to the problem feeling strong and light. On his first few attempts, he nearly stuck the crux move but each time he fumbled the left hand crimp. Scolding himself for his lack of accuracy, Moffatt took a short rest. He knew that he would be hitting the hold correctly if it was a pocket. Then an idea dawned on him – Moffatt took out his athletic tape and marked a circle around the sweet spot on the hold. Sure enough this trick worked; Moffatt stuck the first move, held the swing and then sent the rest of the problem. Moffatt named the problem Dominator because of the pure power required and suggested a rating of 8a+/8b. The problem, which has been repeated with several different methods, is now thought to be solid V12.

During the rest of the 90s, Yosemite received a renewed interest in bouldering. Many areas outside of Camp 4, which until now hosted only a few problems, were filled out with fun new moderates. Areas like the Cathedral Boulders began to have circuits that rivaled the Camp 4 circuit. People like Rick Cashner, Dean Potter, and Steve Jenivene searched the Valley floor for great problems and established classics such as Bruce Lee, The King, and The Octagon. In 1998 Lynn Hill made the coveted first female ascent of Midnight Lightning.

By 2000 Yosemite was a world class bouldering area with many classics for all levels of difficulty. In 2002 Chris Sharma completed the obvious sit start to the Dominator, creating Dominated V13. The same year Lisa Rands made the first female ascent of Thriller. In the past few years, Yosemite has continued to see development. Surprisingly, classics are popping up every year even in well established areas like Camp 4. Recently individuals including Randy Puro, Paul Barraza, Tim Medina, Greg Loh, Matt Wilder, and Tommy Caldwell have been combing the woods, finding new gems scattered about the Valley. They have established hard classics such as Scissors for Lefty, Shadow Warrior, and Chimera. Yosemite is showing no signs of becoming climbed out – anyone who has explored the Valley floor knows of at least one boulder lost somewhere in the woods with beautiful features and no trace of chalk. Now it's your chance to make Yosemite bouldering history. Look beyond the established areas – get out there – find, clean, and climb the classic new problems of the future.

The Big Stone.

METOLIUS

Grades and Stars

This guidebook uses the V-scale to rate all boulder problems. Inevitably, there will be disagreements over the grade of a problem and the grades used here represent the best consensus that could be reached. Remember that the grade is just a tool for helping you find problems within your range of ability. Just use them as a guide for finding great problems to try. The stars associated with the problem represent an objective quality rating. Since the climbing experience is subjective, you may often disagree with the stars a problem receives. The goal of including stars is to help you have a sense of how good a problem might be. Some of the

characteristics of a problem that are assessed include: aesthetics of the line and boulder, interest and uniqueness of movement, friendliness of holds, general location and history. The scale is from zero to four stars and is intended to differentiate problems of quality. Thus, a one-star problem can still be interesting and fun. Furthermore, the scale is meant to be a worldwide basis for quality. The purpose of this is to give people a quality rating that they can understand even if they haven't visited the area. For example, imagine a small area that only had a few problems that were mediocre. If the best problems in that area were given four stars, one might think that there are amazing problems there. However, in the context of all the problems in the world, those problems might just be two stars. If the guidebook author used a universal star system, then those problems would be given two stars and a visitor would know what to expect. So, the star system in this book is meant to be universal. It happens that Yosemite has some of the best problems in the world and so a local scale would actually correspond to a global scale. At any rate, the number of stars associated with a problem should give you a good sense of the quality of that problem once you're familiar with the scale. In the inset box on the next page you will find an explanation of what to expect out of each star rating.

Hueco	Y.D.S	Font
VB	5.0-5.8	<3
V0-	5.9	3/4-
V0	5.10a/b	4-/4/4+
V0+	5.10c/d	4+
V1	5.11a/b	4+/5-
V2	5.11b/c	5/5+
V3	5.11c/d	6a/b
V4	5.12a/b	6c/c+
V5	5.12b/c	7a
V6	5.12c/d	7a+
V7	5.13a/b	7a+/7b
V8	5.13b/c	7b/7b+
V9	5.13c/d	7b+/7c
V10	5.14a	7c/7c+
V11	5.14b	7c+/8a
V12	5.14c	8a+
V13	5.14d	8b
V14	5.14d/5.15a	8b+
V15	5.15a/b	8c
V16	5.15b/c	8c+

Breakdown of Stars

★★★★ This problem is amazing. It has most of these qualities: interesting movements, unique holds, an independent line, a beautiful setting, quality rock, and a rich history. You must do this problem if it is within your ability. Four-star problems are somewhat rare gems.

★★★ This is an excellent problem that is similar to a four-star problem except that it has one or two minor elements that detract from it. These could include one or two sharp holds, other problems in the vicinity, a slightly awkward move or a less than perfect setting. Nonetheless, you should definitely seek out and do these problems if you can. Three-star problems are more common but still many areas have just a few or none.

★★ A two-star problem is one that is a lot of fun but is lacking some of the elements that would make it more classic. Usually these problems have one or two really good components such as great movement, interesting holds, or a beautiful line. Two-star problems are very common and most good problems fall into this quality rating.

★ A one-star problem is one that is not that great but has some redeeming value that still makes it worth trying. These problems are not ones that you would typically seek out, but instead are ones that you might still find enjoyment in after you have done the more classic problems of an area. Most of the mediocre problems in the world fall into this rating.

A zero-star problem is typically not worth doing. It doesn't really have anything going for it. However, since climbing is subjective, even a zero-star problem could give you enjoyment. Zero-star problems are the ones that someone did because they were bored, but otherwise they might never have been done.

Alley Dorey on the four-star Midnight Lightning (V8). Photo by Matt Wilder.

Yosemite's Best

Here are the top ten not-to-be-missed problems in Yosemite for three different grade ranges. Page numbers in parentheses.

VB - V4

- ❏ The Presidential Traverse VB (60)
- ❏ The Largo Lunge V0- (118)
- ❏ Great White V1 (84)
- ❏ Circuit Breaker V2 (78)
- ❏ Double Decker V2 (102)
- ❏ Once Upon a Time V3 (48)
- ❏ Get It Up V3 (48)
- ❏ Bachar Cracker V4 (118)
- ❏ The Bates Problem V4 (114)
- ❏ Zorro V4 (80)

V5 - V8

- ❏ Cocaine Corner V5 (131)
- ❏ Crossroad Moe V6 (36)
- ❏ Sentinel Traverse V6 (64)
- ❏ Shiver Me Timbers V6 (134)
- ❏ The Octagon V6 (44)
- ❏ Torque V7 (72)
- ❏ No Holds Bard V7 (64)
- ❏ Midnight Lightning V8 (114)
- ❏ King Cobra V8 (118)
- ❏ The Diamond V8 (58)

V9 - V13

- ❏ Heart of Darkness V9 (148)
- ❏ The Force V9 (120)
- ❏ Sex Factor X V9 (119)
- ❏ Thriller V10 (120)
- ❏ Drive On V10 (87)
- ❏ Across The Tracks V10 (148)
- ❏ Yabo Roof V11 (139)
- ❏ The Dominator V12 (132)
- ❏ Shadow Warrior V12 (58)
- ❏ Dominated V13 (132)

The author gets a bad flapper.

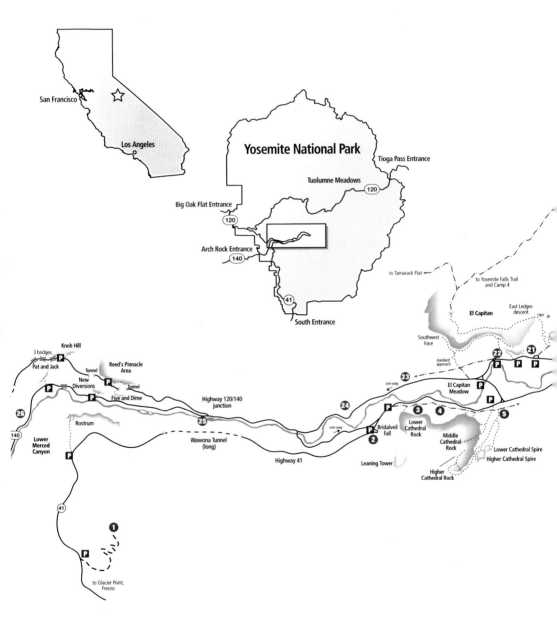

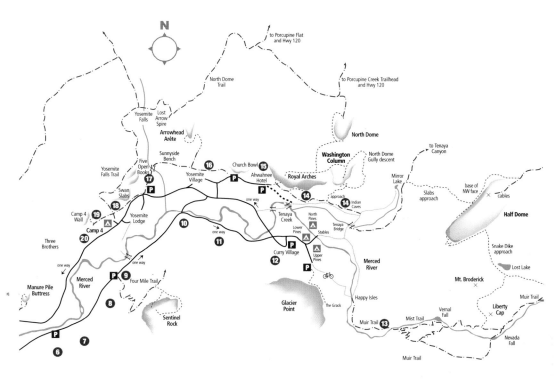

Yosemite Valley Bouldering Areas

How to use this guide

This guide is divided into sections by bouldering area (e.g. Camp 4, The Ahwahnee Boulders, Housekeeping, etc.). Each area in Yosemite usually consists of a condensed collection of boulders that is separated spatially from the other areas. A few areas, however, are adjacent to each other and the border between them can seem arbitrary. Each area receives a section in the book. Larger areas are often divided into subsections (e.g. Camp 4 – East, Camp 4 – Central, etc.) The areas in this guide are ordered by location roughly following a horseshoe shape that starts at the southwest side of the Valley and wraps around to the northwest side. The map on the previous page shows the locations and order of the areas. Each section in the guide consists of an overview of the area that includes parking and approach information, a topo for the area or part of the area, photos of some boulders with lines demarcating the problems, and a description for every problem. Once you arrive in an area, you can locate yourself by trying to find one of the pictured boulders. Find the number of a problem on that photo and then find that number on the topo to determine your location on the map. From here you should have a sense of where you are and should be able to find the rest of the problems. In addition to the photos and topos, every problem in the guide has a description that explains the starting holds and states where to climb. These descriptions can also help you get your bearings. Additionally, the descriptions give you the grade of the problem, a quality rating, and an assessment of possible danger. An '!' is used to warn you about problems that may be dangerous because of a long fall or bad landing. Problems without a '!' may still be very dangerous – use your discretion when selecting problems. For areas without topos, you will be able to locate the problems just using the photos and descriptions. Most of the time, descents are obvious, but some of the trickier descents may be drawn with a black arrow on the topo.

Deciphering the topos

The topos are primarily meant to give you a better sense of the area's spatial layout. Each topo includes additional symbols that help you match the topo to what you see around you. Below is a legend that shows the symbols that will regularly be found on a topo.

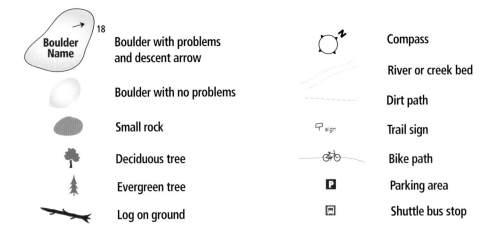

Boulder with problems and descent arrow	Compass
	River or creek bed
Boulder with no problems	Dirt path
Small rock	Trail sign
Deciduous tree	Bike path
Evergreen tree	Parking area
Log on ground	Shuttle bus stop

Turtle Dome

Approach time: **20 minutes**

Number of problems: **10+**

Turtle Dome offers a setting completely different from the other Valley bouldering areas. Located high above the Valley floor, this area more closely resembles Tuolumne bouldering. It is, however, easily accessed from the Valley. There are not too many problems in this area and most are in the easy range. Nonetheless, this area is definitely worth the visit for the ambiance and the views alone.

Approach

Park in a dirt pullout on the right side of Highway 41 south 3.7 miles past the intersection of 140 and 41 (the Bridalveil parking lot). This is 0.4 miles south of the paved parking pullout for the Rostrum. Walk down the road past the pullout (heading south) for about 500 ft. On your left you will see a small dirt road. Follow this road to a gate where the road becomes paved. Hike up the road until you reach the antennae at the summit. The best boulder and view is near the second antenna structure. A direct approach from the Rostrum pullout may be possible.

Bridalveil Boulders

Approach time: **4 minutes**

Number of problems: **14**

This area has a few classics and lots of
potential for quality new problems. Though
in a beautiful setting, this area can be
a bit hectic during peak tourist times.
Fortunately, most of the boulders are set
apart from the main tourist areas.

Approach

The Bridalveil Falls parking lot is located
on the south side of the Valley just west of
where Highway 140 meets Highway 41.

Crossroads Boulder

This is a fun little boulder sitting by itself.
Across the street from the Bridalveil parking
lot is a small pullout lined with boulders.
Head northwest from the west end of this
pullout. You will see the obvious boulder
after about 400 ft.

Bridalveil Falls.

☐ **1. Unnamed V7** ★ Start on Gak and
traverse right to finish on Crossroads Moe.

☐ **2. Gak V0-** ★★
Start on a low
triangle jug. Climb
up using the arête.

☐ **3. Critterfish V0**
★★ Go straight
up from a jug and
a sidepull in the
horizontal at 6 ft.
Finish left.

☐ **4. Crossroads
Moe V6** ★★★ Start
on sloping rail and
climb straight up.
Exit either R or L.

Number of problems by difficulty

VB	V0	V1	V2	V3	V4	V5	V6	V7	V8	V9	V10	≥V11
0	4	0	1	1	2	1	3	2	0	0	0	0

❏ **5. Naked and Hairy Traverse V4** ★ Start on Crossroads Moe and traverse left to finish on Gak.

❏ **6. Little Mouse V3** ★★ Start on chest-high opposing sidepulls. Follow the seam up and left to a straight up finish.

❏ **7. Skatement V6** ★ Climb the faint seam and corner just right of the rock scar. Start high.

Bridalveil Boulders

This section features interesting problems on slightly different rock. Many of the problems still need more cleaning. There are many more boulders above the two mapped here. Many classic new problems are waiting to be uncovered in this cluster. This area is also home to a few crack boulder problems scattered above the first two boulders. Park in the Bridalveil lot and walk past the bathrooms towards the Leaning Tower.

❏ **1. Unnamed V0-** ★ Start with a right hand jug at head height. Go left to another jug and then climb straight up.

❏ **2. Unnamed V2** ★ Reach to a high edge on the face right of the arête. Climb straight up using the arête. Needs cleaning.

❏ **3. Project** Start on angled edges right of the blunt arête. Dyno to a good hold around the arête and then top out.

❏ **4. Unnamed V4** ★★ ! Start high and follow the right angling seam to a high finish.

❏ **5. Unnamed V0** ★ ! Start on a sketchy big block and climb straight up.

❏ **6. Unnamed V5** ★★ Start sitting with good underclings. Follow the seam leftwards to a finish with the tree at your back.

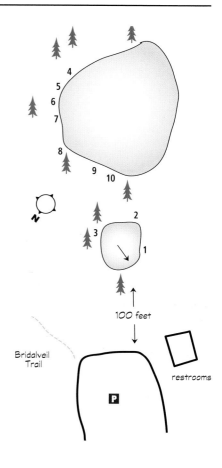

❏ **7. Unnamed V6** ★ Start on the left side of the big white flake. Go rightwards and up.

❏ **8. Unnamed V7** ★★ Sit start with a good jug. Climb up to a big undercling and then continue up and left.

❏ **9. Project** Start with a high right hand sidepull. Go up to a black crimp and then keep going straight up.

❏ **10. Project** Sit start with a slopey hold

Lower Cathedral

Approach time: **2 minutes**

Number of problems: **1+**

Lower Cathedral Rock contains some of the most interesting rock in the Valley. There are not too many boulders below this cliff and very few have been developed. Perhaps there is good potential though for interesting problems on unique rock. There is one boulder close to the road that has a classic crack/face climb and potential for more good problems..

Approach

After the Bridalveil parking lot, when you are traveling into the Valley, there is a straight section of road that has a paved pullout on each side of the road (and a nice view of El Cap). After these pullouts, there are three paved pullouts on the left in succession. Park in the third pullout which is 0.5 m past the Bridalveil parking lot. Cross the road and hike up the right side of a steep bank. The boulder is about 200 ft. slightly to the left if you are looking at Lower Cathedral Rock.

❏ **1. Do-Bop V7 ★★★** ! Climb the zigzag crack on the wall that faces Middle Cathedral (east). Start standing, go right, then up, then left, and finally up again at the end.

Dean Potter on the Wizard (V10). Photo by Dean Fidelman

Gunsight Boulders

Approach time: **3 minutes**

Number of problems: **9**

This small area is home to a few problems. The Bionic Traverse, which features big slopey fine-grained grey granite holds, is probably the most worthy problem in the group.

Approach

Park in a paved turnout on the left 0.7 miles past where Highway 140 meets Highway 41 (near the Bridalveil Falls parking lot). This turnout comes just before a big boulder that sits just to the right of the road.

Speedway Boulder

This boulder is visible from the road and located just west of the turnout.

❏ **1. Unnamed V1** ★ Climb the face left of the corner.

❏ **2. Billy in the Well Low V7** ★ Start sitting to the left of Billy in the Well and climb into and up it.

❏ **3. Billy in the Well V4** ★ Reach high crimps and then mantel.

❏ **4. Yosemite Speedway Traverse V7** ★ Start on #3 and traverse right on the lip to a step off onto the big flake below the boulder.

❏ **5. Unnamed V1** Grab the jug and top out.

❏ **6. Unnamed V2** ★ Grab edges, go to the lip and then top out.

❏ **7. Road Rage V5** ★ Mantel at the shallow left-facing corner.

❏ **8. Unnamed V0** ★ Start on jugs above the big flake. Traverse left a bit and then top out.

Bionic Boulder

There is a cluster of boulders near the trail 300 ft. west of the Speedway Boulder. This boulder is uphill from the trail. The problem faces away from the trail.

❏ **9. Bionic Traverse V5** ★★ Traverse the south face of this boulder. Start sitting near the left side with good holds. Go all the way right and then top out.

Cathedral Boulders

Approach time: **5-10 minutes**

Number of problems: **67**

This is one of the most condensed areas in Yosemite. You will find fun problems of all levels on tight-grained featured rock. This guide divides this area into two sectors: The Hex Sector and The King Sector.

Approach

Park at the turnout just before the road to El Cap bridge, or park where the road from El Cap bridge meets the south side drive. Follow a trail into the woods that leads to the main foot path that parallels the road. From here follow a worn trail towards Higher Cathedral Rock. After about 1000 ft. you will see the boulders left of the trail.

Matt Wilder on The King (V7).
Photo by Chris McNamara

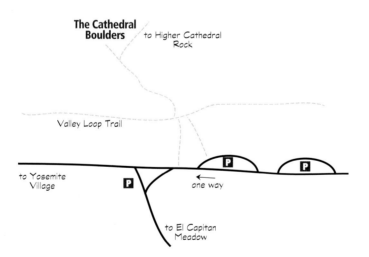

The Cathedral
Boulders

to Higher Cathedral
Rock

Valley Loop Trail

P

P

P

to Yosemite
Village

←
one way

to El Capitan
Meadow

Number of problems by difficulty

VB	V0	V1	V2	V3	V4	V5	V6	V7	V8	V9	V10	≥V11
8	15	4	6	8	7	6	3	6	2	0	2	0

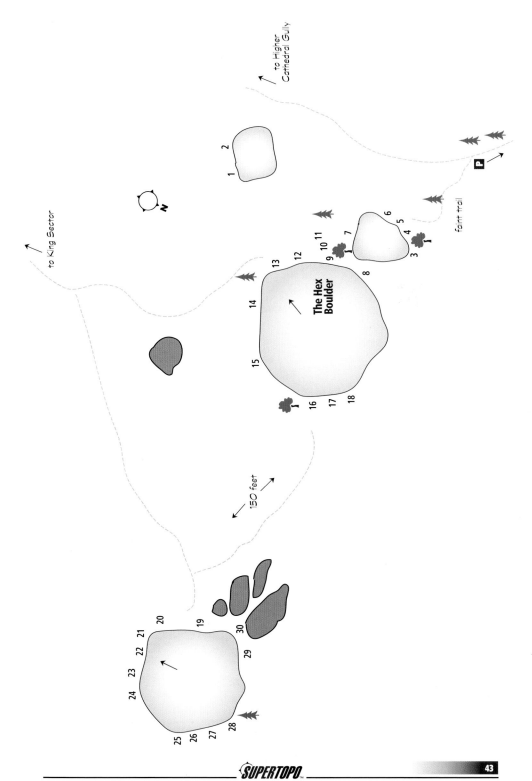

Trail Boulder

❏ **1. Unnamed V2** ★ Sit start on right-facing sidepulls. Dyno to a jug and continue to the top.

❏ **2. Unnamed VB** ★ Start with a positive edge at 6 ft. Climb straight up.

❏ **3. Unnamed VB** ★ Climb the face left of the tree.

❏ **4. Bi-Focal V0** ★★ Climb the face above the waist-high shelf.

❏ **5. What's Next V3** ★★ Start on high holds. Climb up and left following the arête / seam.

❏ **6. The Bogart Traverse V5** ★★ Start on What's Next and traverse right on good holds below the lip to a mantel around the corner.

❏ **7. Fish Head V7** ★★ Sit start with a good hold. Climb straight up the blunt arête.

The Hex Boulder

❏ **8. Unnamed V5** ★ ! Start with a high jug. Climb up and right to the finish of The Hexcentric.

❏ **9. The Hexcentric V7** ★★★ ! Start on high crimps and go straight up. (Sit start V7).

❏ **10. Octagon Traverse V8** ★ ! Sit start The Hexcentric and climb right to finish on The Octagon.

❏ **11. Fat Man Traverse V7** ★ Start on the Octagon Traverse and continue right to finish on the end of Ladder Detail.

❏ **12. The Octagon V6** ★★★ ! Start on high crimps and climb straight up past a sloping rail to the top.

❏ **13. Ladder Detail V5** ★★ Sit start with a jug at the arête. Make a long move to a sloper and then climb to better holds. (Stand start VB).

❏ **14. Clean Up V0** Climb the face below a bulging section from a high start.

❏ **15. Who Knows V3** ★★ Start on a big slopey rail at 4 ft. Climb left and up through the bulge.

❏ **16. Project** Start from a high crimp and climb straight up.

❏ **17. "X" V10** ★★★ ! Start standing with a left hand crimp and an angled right hand hold under the roof. Climb up and right through tricky moves.

❏ **18. Hard Headed Arête V1** ★★ ! Climb the right arête to join the finish of "X."

The Cathedral Boulder

❏ **19. The Wizard V10** ★★ ! Start on nearby boulders. Jump to 10 ft. high edges in the middle of the face. Then climb straight up.

❏ **20. The Cathedral Problem V5** ★★ ! Climb the left side of the arête from a high start.

❏ **21. Herb V3** ★ ! Climb the right side of the arête.

❏ **22. Gunsight VB** ★★ ! Start near the left side of the face and climb up and right to good holds through the center of the face.

❏ **23. Ray D'Arcy Memorial Problem V3** ★ Start with a head-height crimp in the middle of the face. Go up and left to join Gunsight.

❏ **24. Toe Licker V8** ★★ Start with a right hand sidepull crimp and a left hand sloper. Slap up the blunt angled arête.

❏ **25. Full Sail V7** ★★ ! Climb straight up the slab just right of the blank left leaning arête.

❏ **26. Norma V4** ★★ Start on Full Sail, climb rightwards to better holds, and then finish up the K-Y Problem.

❏ **27. K-Y Problem V3** ★ Start on a high left-facing sidepull. Go straight up.

❏ **28. Shaggy V2** ★ ! Climb straight up the broken seam at the arête.

❏ **29. Project** Climb the steep faint arête.

❏ **30. Project** Climb the left arête above a bad landing.

Yeah! Boulder

❏ **1. Peyote V5 ★ !** Start just right of the rock at the base. Climb up the face using the hole and the right-facing flake.

❏ **2. Without a Fro V3 ★** Start on crimps on the face. Go up and then right to the face.

❏ **3. La Jolla Arête V0+ ★** Climb the blunt arête just left of the thin tree.

❏ **4. Green Face VB ★** Go straight up the center of the face.

❏ **5. Unnamed V0 ★** Climb the arête starting with a sloper and a crimp.

❏ **6. Unnamed V2 ★** Start on a left-facing crimp at 5 ft. and go up and left.

❏ **7. Unnamed V2 ★** Climb the left-angling arête from a high start.

❏ **8. Bingo V0 ★** Climb the slab without using the arête.

❏ **9. Unnamed V0 ★** Climb the face starting at an indentation in the arête.

❏ **10. Yeah! V0 ★★** Start on high jugs. Go right and up.

❏ **11. Yeah! Sit V2 ★★** Sit start to Yeah!.

Misc Boulders

❏ **12. Scrubby V0** Climb the mossy slab in a variety of places.

❏ **13. Project** Climb the left-facing feature.

❏ **14. Spire Traverse V6 ★** Start on left side of face. Traverse to the right with your hands usually 6 to 8 ft. off the ground. Finish on the right side of the face around the corner.

❏ **15. Unnamed V4 ★** Sit start with a positive edge. Dyno to slopers and then top out.

❏ **16. Mambo V1 ★** Stand start. Climb arête.

❏ **17. Unnamed VB ★★** Climb the easiest part of the slab.

❏ **18. Serendipity V1** Climb the slab 5 ft. left of the tree.

❏ **19. Unnamed V0 ★★** Jump start to a jug and then go left and up.

The King Boulder

❏ **20. Unnamed VB** ★ Climb the broken wide arête.

❏ **21. Feels Like an Oil Slick V4** ★ Sit start with edges. Traverse right to finish on The King's Throne.

❏ **22. Crippler V4** ★★ ! Start on Feels Like an Oil Slick and climb straight up.

❏ **23. St. Louis Variation V6** ★ ! Start sitting with low slopers 6 ft. right of Feels Like an Oil Slick. Traverse left to finish on Crippler.

❏ **24. The King's Throne V0** ★★ ! Mantel the shelf and then top out.

❏ **25. Project** Climb the faint left-facing feature.

❏ **26. So Good V5** ★★★ ! Start on a big undercling at head height. Go right and up through edges and slopers.

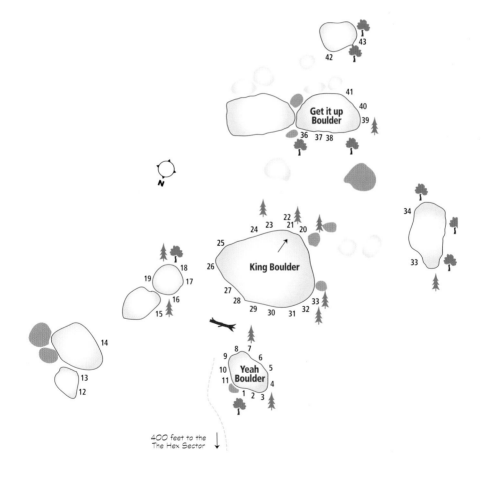

❏ **27. Behave V7 ★★** ! Jump start to a high flat edge. Climb straight up.

❏ **28. The King V7 ★★★** Start with a good left hand sidepull. Climb leftwards along the lip to a mantel at the apex. (V7 if you escape early onto the slab).

❏ **29. White Dike V4 ★** ! Climb the white dike just right of the arête from a high start.

❏ **30. Break a Leg V1 ★** ! Climb the shelfy face 4 ft. left of the tree.

❏ **31. Did It Up V4 ★★** ! Start on high angled crimps. Climb up and then right.

❏ **32. Wreaker V2 ★** ! Climb left-angling arête.

❏ **33. Unnamed V0 ★** High start. Climb groove.

❏ **34. Teva VB ★** Start on a blocky jug and climb straight up.

❏ **35. Scoopy V0** Climb the mossy scoop. Would be good if it was cleaned well.

Get It Up Boulder

❏ **36. Get It Longer V4 ★** ! Start above the angled tree. Traverse right into Get It Up.

❏ **37. Get It Up V3 ★★★** ! Start on jugs in front of the pine tree. Go up and right on jugs to a high finish.

❏ **38. Grand Larceny V5 ★★** ! Start on Get It Up. Go right along the high horizontal crack.

❏ **39. Unnamed V0-** Climb the slab directly above the pine tree.

❏ **40. Unnamed V0 ★** Start on an angled edge in the bulge. Go right to a crimp in the crack and then climb straight up.

❏ **41. Unnamed VB ★** Start in cracks on the right side. Traverse left on the horizontal crack to a finish.

❏ **42. Project** Bear hug your way up arête.

❏ **43. Jonesin' V3 ★★** Start with a high right-facing sidepull on the arête. Climb straight up.

Chris McNamara on Octagon (V7). Photo by Lincoln Else.

Lost Boulders

Approach time: 5-15 minutes

Number of problems: **17**

This more obscure area can be a fun adventure when you are sick of the standard areas. The highlights for the area are definitely the crack problems. The Cedar Crack offers some good suffering through a steep offwidth corner. Deliverance is a beautiful hard steep splitter that starts with tight hands and pinches down to fingers.

Approach

Park in a dirt pullout on the left lined with rocks 0.5 miles after the point where El Cap bridge road meets south side drive. Hike straight uphill (no trail) until you get to the horse trail. Go left (east) on this trail for a few hundred feet. Soon you will see a big boulder on your right about 80 ft. from the trail; this is the Cedar Boulder.

To Be Someone Boulder

❏ **1. To Be Someone V4** ★★ Start on high small crimps and climb straight up.

❏ **2. Wanna Be V3** ★ Climb the arête past an undercling.

❏ **3. Unnamed VB** ★ Climb the arête.

❏ **4. Unnamed V0** ★★ Climb the left-facing feature.

❏ **5. Unnamed V0-** ★ Climb the right side of the face.

Deliverence (V8).

Cedar Boulder

❏ **6. Project** Climb the tall face just right of the chimney.

❏ **7. Project** Climb the arête and then pull onto the high slab.

❏ **8. Miss Laid V2** ★ ! Start standing. Squeeze the V feature. Go with your right hand to a good edge and then mantel.

❏ **9. Cedar Crack V5** ★★ Climb the offwidth crack between the two boulders. Sit start.

❏ **10. Project** Start with the jug on the right face. Climb into the Cedar Crack. The opposite wall is on as soon as it is useful.

❏ **11. Unnamed V3** ★ Traverse the lip from a stand start at the right side. Finish where the two boulders meet.

Number of problems by difficulty

VB	V0	V1	V2	V3	V4	V5	V6	V7	V8	V9	V10	≥V11
2	4	2	1	2	2	2	1	0	1	0	0	0

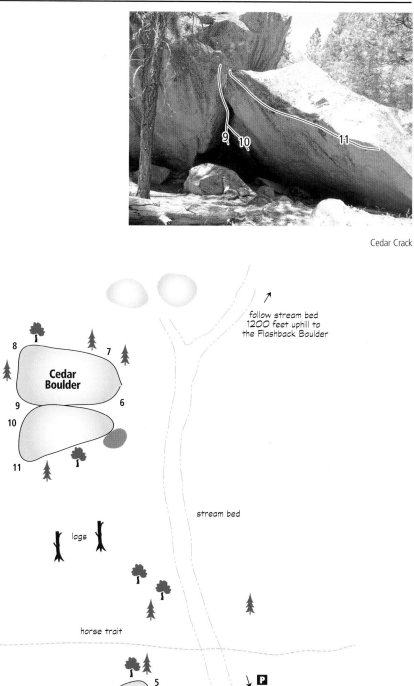

Cedar Crack

follow stream bed
1200 feet uphill to
the Flashback Boulder

**Cedar
Boulder**

stream bed

logs

N

horse trail

P

Flashback Boulder

Hike up the stream bed from the Cedar Boulder. After about 1200 ft. the stream bed gets wider with bigger boulders. This boulder is on the right side and is distinguished by an orange lichen spot facing the stream bed.

❏ **1. Project** Climb the juggy face between the two trees.

❏ **2. Project** Climb the right-facing seams and edges.

❏ **3. Project** Climb the right-facing corner.

❏ **4. Unnamed V5** ★★ ! Start standing just left of the sloping shelf. Climb straight up past a left-angling undercling/seam.

❏ **5. Unnamed V4** ★ ! Start on #4 and climb up and right to finish just left of the arête.

❏ **6. Unnamed V0** ★ ! Climb the face past a horizontal slot.

Flashback Boulder

❏ **7. Unnamed V0** ★ Start with a high crimp below the right-angling shelf. Climb up and right.

❏ **8. Flashback V1** ★ Climb the left-facing seam. This would be more classic with more cleaning.

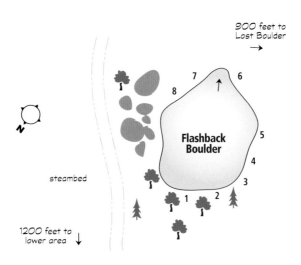

The Lost Boulder

From the Flashback Boulder, hike west across the hill staying at the same height. After about 900 ft., you will see some boulders just past a clearing. The bottom boulder has some good projects; the top boulder is the Lost Boulder.

❏ **1. Unnamed VB** ★ Climb the chimney.

❏ **2. Project** Climb the arête and face just right of the chimney.

❏ **3. Project** Climb the arête to a juggy rail that leads left.

❏ **4. Project** Climb up the face just right of the tree.

❏ **5. Unnamed V1** ★★ ! Climb the crack to a high topout.

❏ **6. The Other Crack V6** ★ Start sitting and climb the tips splitter just right of the pine tree.

❏ **7. Deliverance V8** ★★★ Start sitting with tight hand jams in the middle of the roof. Climb the thinning crack to a tight finish. (If you're interested, you can start deeper and make this a real butt dragger).

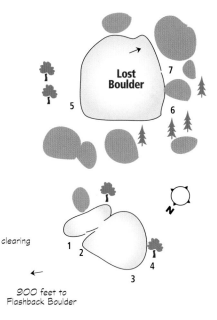

Candyland

Approach time: **7 minutes**

Number of problems: **27**

This new area is home to some modern classics. It's a bit more isolated than most of the other areas and provides a unique view of El Capitan. Once Upon a Time V3 is an amazing stemming problem that is not to be missed. For some harder classics, don't miss the Diamond Boulder.

Approach

Park at a dirt pullout on the left 0.6 miles after the intersection of El Cap Bridge road and South Side Drive – this is the second dirt pullout on the left after a paved pullout with two big trees growing out of the pavement. From the pullout, hike straight uphill to the Horse Trail. At this point on the trail, there is a cut log that crosses the trail. The boulders are about five minutes straight uphill from this log. A faint trail leads up, left, and then back right from the left (east) side of this log.

❏ **1. Unnamed V0** ★ Start with a left hand sidepull jug and a right hand sidepull crimp. Go to the lip and then mantel to the right.

The Storybook Boulder

❏ **2. Unnamed V0** ★ Sit start with jugs left of the downclimb. Traverse left along the juggy shelf. There are several topout possibilities. The straight up can also be climbed.

Matt Wilder on Changing Corners (V8).
Photo by Chris McNamara

❏ **3. Once Upon a Time V3** ★★★★ ! Climb the dihedral from a stand start.

❏ **4. Reading Backwards V4** ★★ Do the first move of Happily Ever After and then traverse left to finish on Once Upon a Time.

❏ **5. Happily Ever After V6** ★★★ Climb the arête from a sit start.

Number of problems by difficulty

VB	V0	V1	V2	V3	V4	V5	V6	V7	V8	V9	V10	≥V11
2	6	0	2	4	5	2	3	0	2	1	0	1

Lyn Verinsky on Once Upon a Time (V3). Photo by Matt Wilder.

❏ **6. Pushover V0 ★★** ! Start on high holds at the left side of the shelf. Climb straight up.

❏ **7. Final Departure V5 ★★** ! Start on Pushover and traverse right along the shelf to a finish near A Land Far Away.

❏ **8. Project** Start on A Land Far Away and climb up and left to the slopey shelf. Then finish on Final Departure.

❏ **9. A Land Far Away V3 ★★★** ! Start with two slopey jugs. Go up and slightly right to a slopey rail. Then climb up and left to the top.

Kudra Boulder

❏ **10. Alobar V2 ★** Start on a jug at the left side of the boulder. Climb up to the angled edge rail and then continue to the top.

❏ **11. Jitterbug V9 ★★** Start on Alobar and traverse right into and up Kudra.

❏ **12. Project** Start in the middle of the face and climb up and slightly left to a finish just right of Alobar.

❏ **13. Kudra V6 ★★** ! Start standing with right-facing edges. Climb straight up using the arête with your right hand.

❏ **14. Project** Climb the steep prow.

❏ **15. Project** Start sitting at the right side of the face. Climb left to a mantel with the tree at your back.

❏ **16. Two-Tier V0 ★★** Start on the slab. Climb up and left past the capstone.

❏ **17. Unnamed VB ★** Climb the slabby rounded arête.

❏ **18. Unnamed V3 ★** Climb the arête from a sit.

❏ **19. Unnamed V0** Climb the left side of the face.

❏ **20. Project** Climb the right side of the middle of the face.

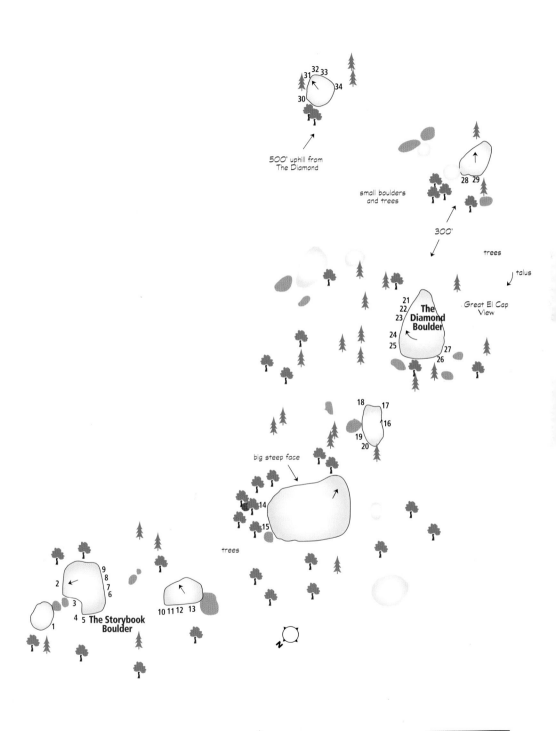

31 32 33
30 34

500' uphill from
The Diamond

small boulders
and trees

28 29

300'

trees

talus

Great El Cap
View

21
22
23
**The
Diamond
Boulder**
24
25
27
26

18 17
16
19
20

big steep face

14
16
15

trees

9
8
2 7
6
3
4 5 **The Storybook
Boulder**
10 11 12 13
1

N

The Diamond Boulder

❏ **21. The Shadow Warrior V12 ★★★★** Start standing with a good holds below the faint corner. Climb out to good holds near the point of the prow and then mantel.

❏ **22. The Ruff V5 ★** Start with one hand in the faint dihedral and one had on a crimp to the right. Climb straight up.

❏ **23. Unnamed V0 ★ !** Reach to a high jug and climb straight up.

❏ **26. The Diamond Left V6 ★★** Start on the Diamond and exit left when you get to the arête.

❏ **25. The Diamond V8 ★★★** Start sitting with an angled crimp rail. Go up to a crimp and then lunge left to the right-leaning rail. Reach to the arête and then follow the arête to the point.

❏ **26. The Changing Corners V8 ★★★ !** Climb the finned arête from a stand start.

❏ **27. Project** Start on The Changing Corners and climb right into the obtuse dihedral. This has a bad landing, but will be classic climbing.

❏ **28. Mickey Mouse Traverse V4 ★★** Start on the left side with angled sloping jugs. Traverse right around the corner and then follow crimps to the topout.

❏ **29. Mickey Mouse Extension V5 ★★** Start on the Mickey Mouse Traverse and continue traversing until you reach the slab.

❏ **30. The Millionth Try V4 ★★** Climb the arête from a sit start.

❏ **31. Unnamed VB ★** Climb right of the groove from a stand start.

❏ **32. Unnamed V2 ★★ !** Start standing with edges left of the dihedral. Climb straight up.

❏ **33. Unnamed V4 ★★ !** Start on the previous problem and climb left to join the The James Memorial Problem.

❏ **34. The James Memorial Problem V3 ★★★** Climb the jagged arête from a sit start.

Matt Wilder on Shadow Warrior (V12). Photo by Noah Kaufman.

Presidential Boulder

Approach time: **2 minutes**

Number of problems: **7**

This boulder probably has the best easy bouldering in the Valley. It features a 35-foot-long, 14-foot-high slab littered with holds. This is definitely a cool boulder to check out. This boulder is also known as The Kneeling Snow Pig.

Approach

Park at a double-sided paved pullout 1.1 miles past the junction of south side drive and the El Cap bridge road. Follow the road east for about 250 ft. and then head right shortly before the road curves left. Hike straight uphill through a clearing to the horse trail. When you reach the horse trail there are two boulders next to the trail. One is on the north side of the trail, east of where you want to hike up. The other is on the south side of the trail, west of where you want to hike up. Hike uphill from between these two boulders to a big boulder just barely visible from the trail.

❏ **1. The Presidential Traverse V0 ★★★★**
Traverse the featured slab in either direction.

❏ **2. The Presidential VB ★★★★** Climb any straight up problem on this face. It's all classic. The difficulty ranges from 5.3 to 5.9.

❏ **3. Unnamed VB ★★** Climb the slab past a small roof.

❏ **5. Unnamed V0 ★** Climb the right-angling arête from a stand start.

❏ **5. Unnamed V1 ★ !** Climb just right of the pine tree starting with a right-facing feature at 5 ft.

❏ **6. Unnamed V1 ★** Reach high to underclings and then climb straight up.

❏ **7. Cave Direct V4 ★** Jump start to a jug and then climb straight up.

❏ **8. Project** Start on a 6 ft. high edge right of Cave Direct. Climb left to join Cave Direct.

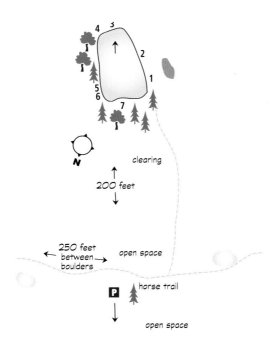

Sentinel Boulders

Approach time: **1 minute**

Number of problems: **37**

This area hosts many fun, easy problems. It is also one of the denser areas for classic mid-range problems (V4 to V8). For a good pump, run laps on the classic Sentinel Traverse.

Approach

Park at the trailhead for the Four Mile Trail. This is a double-sided paved pullout 1.6 miles after the intersection of the El Cap bridge road and South Side Drive. Follow the obvious paved trail south towards Sentinel Rock. The B-1 boulder is the first big boulder on your left where the trail jags right.

Lincoln Else on Sentinel Traverse (V6).
Photo by Chris McNamara

Number of problems by difficulty

VB	V0	V1	V2	V3	V4	V5	V6	V7	V8	V9	V10	≥V11
5	8	3	0	5	3	4	4	3	2	0	0	0

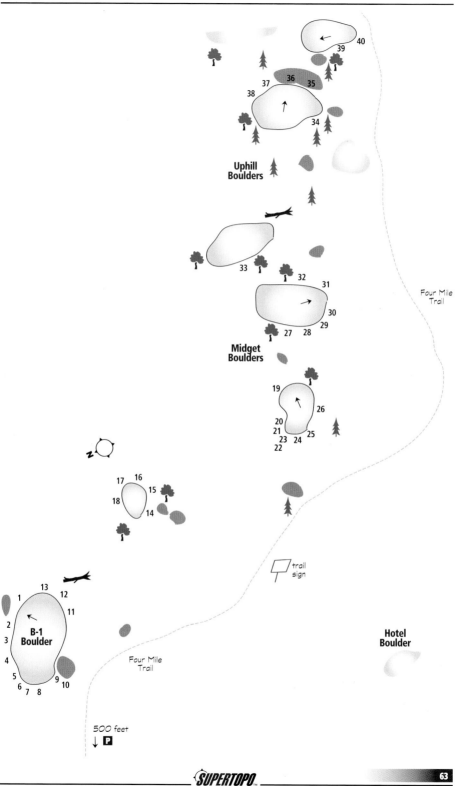

40
39
37
36
35
38
34

Uphill Boulders

33
32
31
30
29
28
27

Midget Boulders

19
26
20
21
25
23 24
22

N

17 16
15
18
14

trail sign

Four Mile Trail

13
1 12
11
2
B-1 Boulder
3
4
5 9
6 7 8 10

Four Mile Trail

Hotel Boulder

500 feet
↓ P

B-1 Boulder

❑ **1. Unnamed** V0 Climb the log to get to the descent ramp.

❑ **2. Jungle Book** V6 ★★ Start with a high left hand sidepull crimp. Make a big move up and right to the left-facing flake. Continue straight up.

❑ **3. No Holds Bard** V7 ★★★ ! Start on high left-facing holds. Climb straight up following the white dike.

❑ **4. Slapshot** V8 ★★ ! Climb the seam from a stand start.

❑ **5. Flake Out** V7 ★★ ! Start on high crimps, climb up and right to an angled shelf, and then top out straight up.

❑ **6. The Abstrusion** V4 ★★ ! Start with a left hand undercling and a right hand sidepull both at head height. Climb up and right.

❑ **7. The Slopster** V6 ★★ ! Start sitting on the boulder at the base. Climb up and slightly right through sloping jugs. (V5 from the stand start).

❑ **8. Unnamed** V5 ★★ Start on a high jug in the middle of the cave. Climb straight up.

❑ **9. Sentinel Traverse** V6 ★★★ Start sitting at the left side of the face with opposing sidepulls. Traverse 25 ft. right to a drop-off at a good jug.

❑ **10. Project** Climb the Sentinel Traverse and then top out.

❑ **11. Project** Climb the smoke-stained overhanging face.

❑ **12. It Seams So** V8 ★ ! Start low with opposing pinches. Follow the seam to the mossy slab. Traverse right to finish up the arête.

❑ **13. South Arête** V1 ★ ! Climb the arête from a high start off of the log.

❑ **14. Unnamed** VB ★ Right-facing corner.

❑ **15. Unnamed** V3 ★ Start on high crimp. Move to a jug.

❑ **16. Unnamed** V0 ★★ Start on a sloper and a sidepull crimp. Climb straight up.

❑ **17. Unnamed** V0+ ★★ Start on jugs at 6 1/2 ft. at the right side of the seam. Traverse left to finish on #15.

❑ **18. Unnamed** V5 ★ Start with a 4 foot high jug. Traverse left on slopers to join #17.

Midget Boulders

❏ **19. Unnamed VB** ★ Climb the prow from a high start.

❏ **20. Unnamed V1** ★ Start on the jug and climb leftwards past a crimp.

❏ **21. Unnamed V0-** ★ Start on the jug and go straight up.

❏ **22. Door Knocker Traverse V3** ★ Start on Door Knocker and traverse up and left into #20.

❏ **23. Door Knocker V0** ★★ Climb the arête from a sit start.

❏ **24. Joby Face V0+** ★ Climb the face left of the juggy shelf at 6 ft.

❏ **25. Unnamed VB** ★ Climb straight up from the right side of the juggy shelf.

❏ **26. Unnamed VB** ★ Climb the slabby scoop.

❏ **27. Unnamed V0** ★ Climb the face 5 ft. right of the tree. Start on high underclings.

❏ **28. Mr. Pink Eyes V0** ★★★ Jump start to a sloping jug above a sloper. Go straight up.

❏ **29. Unnamed V4** ★★ Start with a low sidepull and undercling. Climb straight up the arête.

❏ **30. Midget Traverse V3** ★★ Start high at the arête. Traverse the shelf and then the crack. Mantel 7 ft. right of the tree.

❏ **31. Unnamed V1** ★ Climb the face just right of the arête.

❏ **32. Unnamed V3** ★★ Sit start with jugs 4 ft. left of the tree. Climb up and slightly right.

Uphill Boulders

❏ **33. The Lone Ranger V3**
Climb the short face starting
with a sidepull crimp.

❏ **34. Unnamed V5 ★★ !** Start
on high edges just left of the
boulder. Go up, then left, and
then straight up at the top.

❏ **35. Unnamed V5 ★★** Climb
the left-facing feature from a
shoulder-height start.

❏ **36. Spanish Left V4 ★★★**
Start from the boulder below
with a shoulder-height jug.
Climb up and right.

❏ **37. Spanish Fly V6 ★★★** Start standing
at ground level with a left hand crimp and
a right hand sidepull sloper. Follow the
features left to a top out in the groove.

❏ **38. Spanish Right V7 ★★** Sit start the arête
and climb left into Spanish Fly.

❏ **39. Project** Climb the corner/arête.

❏ **40. Unnamed VB ★★ !** Climb the right
arête.

Cedar Wright on The Sentinel Traverse (V6). Photo by Dean Fidelman.

Chicken Boulder

Approach time: 3 minutes

Number of problems: 7

This individual boulder has a few high easy problems.

Approach

Park at the Sentinel Bridge. Walk west on South Side Drive till you reach the chapel parking lot. Follow the trail that leads off from the far end of the parking lot and travels east of the chapel. After about 250 ft. you will see the boulder on your left. This boulder is usually surrounded by water during the spring and early summer.

❏ **1. Unnamed VB** ! Climb the face left of the tree.

❏ **2. Unnamed V0** ! Climb the arête right of the tree.

❏ **3. Unnamed V2** ★★ ! Climb straight up to the shallow right-facing corner.

❏ **4. Unnamed V2** ★ Climb the main corner.

❏ **5. Unnamed V4** ★ ! Climb the face 6 ft. right of the corner.

❏ **6. Unnamed V1** ★★ ! Climb the faint arête past a horizontal seam. Start from a high jug.

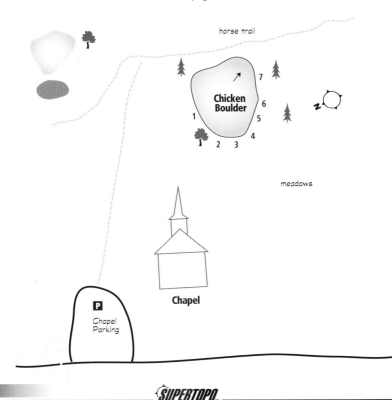

Housekeeping

Matt Keebler on Atheletes Die Young (V5).
Photo by Scott Chandler

Approach time: **30 seconds**

Number of problems: **52**

These boulders offer a good collection of easier problems that are not too high. This area is also hosts Yosemite's hardest finger crack problem, Sasquatch. Park across from the Housekeeping campground in front of the LeConte Memorial building – a small stone building with peaked roofs. The big boulder to the left is the LeConte Boulder.

Approach

Park in the lot in front of the LeConte Memorial (this is also a shuttle bus stop). The big boulder in front of you is the LeConte Boulder.

Athletes Die Young

❏ **1. Darth Maul (a.ka. Lifeline) V10 ★★**
Start on the low jug right of where the two boulders pinch together. Climb up and right to a high topout or jump to the jug on the opposite wall. Variation (Doner V8): Start to the right with a very high right hand edge and left hand undercling pinch. Climb left into Darth Maul. The stand start is V7.

❏ **2. Flatline V8 ★★★** Start with edges in a V at 6 ft. Climb straight up to the middle of the face and then exit up and right on edges.

❏ **3. Heart Attack V6 ★★** Start 10ft. right of Flatline. Climb up to the big undercling and then move left to finish on Flatline.

❏ **4. Guerneys Gone Wild V4 ★★** Climb the bulge to a hard mantel.

❏ **5. Unnamed V1 ★★** Start with the big slopey undercling. Go up to a good edge and then top out.

❏ **6. Unnamed V1** Start on the big jug/shelf. Climb up and left to mantel.

❏ **7. Project** Start at the arête and traverse left to finish on #6.

❏ **8. Atheletes Die Young V5 ★★** Start with a shoulder-height left hand hold and a lower right hand hold. Follow the prow to the top.

❏ **9. Conan V9★★** Sit start at the arête. Climb up and right through small crimps to better holds just below the lip.

❏ **10. Cashner-u-al V4 ★** Start with a right hand diagonal undercling crimp just left of a little rock at the base. Climb straight up.

❏ **11. The Shield V11 ★★** ! Climb the blunt arête from a high squeezing start.

Number of problems by difficulty

VB	V0	V1	V2	V3	V4	V5	V6	V7	V8	V9	V10	≥V11
0	22	2	2	5	6	2	1	3	4	2	2	2

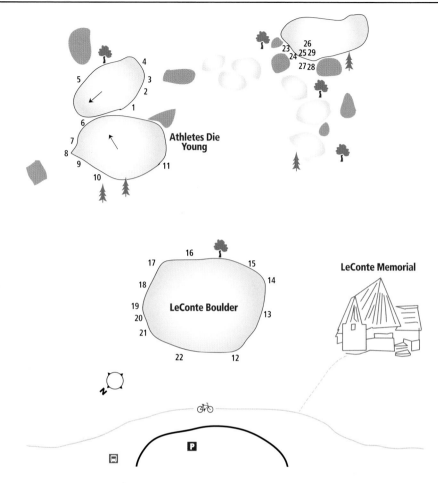

Athletes Die Young

LeConte Boulder

LeConte Memorial

LeConte Boulder

☐ **12. Descent Route V0 ★ !** Climb the crack from a high start. Harder if you start lower.

☐ **13. Kor Practice Aid Ladder A1**

☐ **14. Project** Start on a high jug. Climb up and left on a tall arête.

☐ **15. The Hooker A1**

☐ **16. Sasquatch ★★★ !** Climb the pin scarred crack from a high stand start.

☐ **17. Piranha V9 ★★ !** Start on a high undercling at the arête. Follow the sloping lip left to a mantel near the seam.

☐ **18. Amazon Face V4 ★★★ !** Start directly below the peak of the triangle. Climb up the face.

☐ **19. Unnamed V0 ★ !** Climb up and right through flakes. Go up and right on the slab.

☐ **20. Unnamed V0+ ★ !** Climb the lieback seam. Finish on #19.

☐ **21. Unnamed V3 ★ !** Climb the slab anywhere. This used to be cleaner and more pleasant.

☐ **22. Shuttle Face V2★★ !** Climb the faint corner. Finish up and left up the high slab or downclimb and drop off.

☐ **23. Fine Line V7 ★★ !** Climb the crack from a stand start with your right hand on a sidepull undercling.

☐ **24. Rabbit Habit V8 ★★ !** Start with a high right hand jug. Make a large move left and then continue straight up.

☐ **25. Narcissus V11 ★★★ !** Start under the roof with both hands in the slot. Climb out the roof to join Rabbit Habbit.

☐ **26. Goldmund V10 ★★★ !** Start under roof with a right hand slot and a left hand pinch. Climb into Prowess.

☐ **27. Prowess V7 ★★★ !** Start squeezing the prow with a right hand crimp and a left hand rail. Climb straight up.

☐ **28. Torque V7 ★★★ !** Start on a seven-foot-high jug on the right face. Climb up and left through slopers to a crack finish back right.

☐ **29. Project** Start on Narcissus and climb straight out the roof to join Torque.

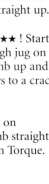

Lyn Verinsky on Torque (V7). Photo by Tim Medina

5. Unnamed V0 ★ Start at the angled corner and traverse the lip rightwards to finish on #7.

6. Unnamed V4 ★★ Start sitting with an edge and a sidepull. Dyno to the lip and then mantel.

7. Cranium Crusher V3★★ Climb the right-facing fin from a sit start.

8. Unnamed V0-★ Climb the face at the shallow left-facing corner.

Pathway Boulders

1. Unnamed V0+ ★★ Traverse #2 to #4.

2. Marco's Edge V0+ ★ Start just right of the tree with a left hand sloper and a right hand sidepull crimp. Go straight up.

3. People Pleaser Face V0 ★★ Start with high angled crimps. Go up and right.

4. Unnamed V0- ★ Climb straight up from high jugs on the right side.

9. Unnamed V4★ Start at the right-facing corner and traverse left along to low lip to finish on #8.

10. Unnamed V0- ★ Climb the arête just left of the right-facing corner.

11. Unnamed V0 ★ Start at the left side and traverse left along the lip.

12. Unnamed V0- ★ Climb the left side of the arête.

13. Unnamed V0 ★ V0 H Climb the arête.

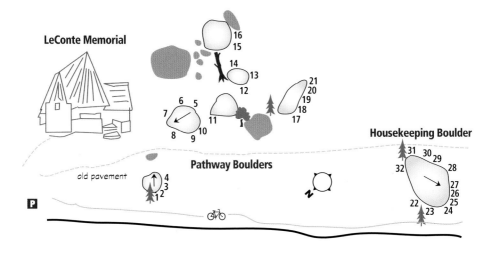

❑ **14. Unnamed V0-** Climb the face above thc base stone.

❑ **15. Project** Climb the arête using edges on the face to the right.

❑ **16. Project** Climb straight up the face from high edges.

The Hidden Loaf

❑ **17. Unnamed V0★** Traverse the lip going either way.

❑ **18. Unnamed V0★** Climb up edges 6 ft. right of the arête.

❑ **19. Collins Direct V8** Climb micro edges in the middle of the face.

❑ **20. Unnamed V3★** Start sitting with your hands at the right side of the rail. Climb leftwards to small crimps and then go to the lip.

❑ **21. Unnamed V0★** Start on the rail, go right to the arête.

The Housekeeping Boulder

❑ **22. Knuckle Fucker V4 ★★** Pull up into the high undercling and then continue straight up.

❑ **23. Trail Traffic V0 ★★** Start with a high right hand undercling and a left hand edge. Go straight up.

❑ **24. Kauk's Crank V5 ★** Start on head-height edges at the arête. Traverse left on slopers to finish on #23.

❑ **25. Unnamed V3 ★** Climb straight up from the start of #24.

❑ **26. Unnamed V0 ★★** Climb the angling shelf on the left side of the slab.

❑ **27. Unnamed V0- ★★ !** Climb the ramp in the middle of the slab.

❑ **28. Unnamed V0 ★★** Climb the arête from a shoulder-height start.

❑ **29. Unnamed V2 ★★** Start on #30 and climb up and right on crimps to the arête.

❑ **30. Purple Barrel V8 ★★** Sit start in the right-facing corner. Go up and right to a crux mantel.

❑ **31. Friction Slab V0+ ★★ !** Start off the boulder at the base and climb the high slab.

❑ **32. The Big Moe V3 ★★** Jump start to a high crimp in the smiley.

Curry Village

Approach time: **2 minutes**

Number of problems: **55**

There is a great collection of boulders spread throughout the Curry Village area. Because it gets more shade, Curry Village is usually one of the cooler places to climb. There are not many super hard lines here, but lots of classic easy problems and moderates.

Approach

Park in any one of the Curry parking lots. See specific approaches for each area.

Curry Village Central

There are many boulders scattered throughout the tent cabin area. A few of the more classic problems are described here. Approach: First find the problem Buckwheat and then walk along the row of cabins to the right (west). To find Buckwheat, walk up the service road left (east) of the mountain shop. As this road curves to the right, you will see a 12-foot-high vertical face up and to the right. This is Buckwheat. It is just left of tent cabin # 321.

❏ **1. Buckweat V4** ★★ Climb the center of the face from a high crimp start.

❏ **2. Unnamed V1** ★★ Just right of cabin #318 is a seam in a corner. Start on a sidepull jug and go straight up.

The next three problems are on the boulder opposite cabin #310.

❏ **3. Unnamed V0** ★★ Climb the slab just right of the tree.

❏ **4. Unnamed VB** ★ Climb the blocky arête.

❏ **5. Unnamed V1** ★ Reach a high crimp and make a long crank up and left.

❏ **6. The Linen Line V1** ★★★ ! Just right of the wooden cabin #292 is a boulder with linen boxes in front of it. Climb into the left-facing corner from a stand start. Then go left to the arête and up. Walk down the back side of the boulder.

❏ **7. The Flapping Shoe V7** ★★ Left of cabin #78 is a featured arête. Start sitting with the sidepull and the shelf. Make challenging moves to gain the better holds up high.

Lisa Davidson on The Angler (V3). Photo by Matt Wilder.

Number of problems by difficulty

VB	V0	V1	V2	V3	V4	V5	V6	V7	V8	V9	V10	≥V11
11	11	5	6	6	6	4	3	0	1	0	0	0

Circuit Breaker

These classic crack problems are at the base of the Staircase Falls rock. Find the wooden cabin #73 in the southwest corner of Curry Village (these are the bigger wooden cabins). Find the trail behind this cabin and follow it uphill. This trail leads directly to the next two problems.

❏ **1. Broken Circuit V5 ★★**
Climb the left of the two cracks. This features thin, off-balance moves.

❏ **2. Circuit Breaker V2 ★★★★** Climb the amazing angled fingercrack up the steep slab.

Curry Vilage - West Side

This cluster of boulders is just past the southwest end of the cabins (near wood cabin #76). It is just uphill from the newer lodging structures.

Root Canal Boulder

❏ **1. Unnamed VB ★★** ! Climb the slab/face just left of the arête.

❏ **2. Unnamed V1 ★★** Climb the arête staying more on the right side.

❏ **3. Project** Sit start with crimps. Climb straight up to jug and then mantel.

❏ **4. Root Canal V7 ★★★** Climb the seam in the corner from a stand start.

❏ **5. Unnamed V1 ★** Climb the arête from a high start. (Low start is a project)

❏ **6. Unnamed V4 ★** Start with a high left hand on arête and low right hand undercling. Climb up and right. (Project: start on the two underclings).

❏ **7. Unnamed V6 ★** Start on the crimps 2 ft. below the lip. Move to the lip and then traverse right to the mantel.

The Angler Boulder

❏ **8. Unnamed VB ★★** Climb the face in a variety of spots.

❏ **9. Unnamed V1 ★★** Start with the right-facing slot in the seam at 6 ft. Climb up and right.

❏ **10. Unnamed V0 ★★** Climb straight up on edges 3 ft. right of the tree.

❏ **11. Unnamed V2 ★★** Start on head-height crimps 7 ft. right of the tree. Climb straight up.

❏ **12. Unnamed V2 ★** Start on #11. Traverse right a few feet and then top out.

❏ **13. Unnamed V6 ★★** Sit start with crimps in a shallow corner at the arête. Climb to the lip and then traverse all the way to finish on The Angler.

❏ **14. Unnamed V2 ★** Pull a mantel starting in the middle of the lip traverse.

❏ **15. The Angler V3 ★★★** Start sitting with diagonal crimps. Climb left to a sloper and a horn. Finish straight up.

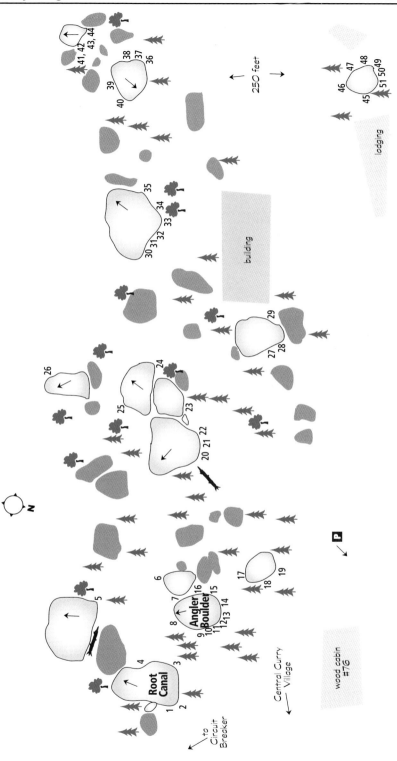

❏ **16. Project** Climb up the faint arête via sharp crimps.

❏ **17. Unnamed V3** ★ Start on low slopers and climb left to the dihedral finish.

❏ **18. Unnamed V1** ★ Jump start to fin and then top out.

❏ **19. Unnamed VB** ★ ! Mantel into the scoop and then climb up.

Kevin's Traverse Boulder

❏ **20. Unnamed V3** ★ Start on low edges and climb straight up to mantel.

❏ **21. Unnamed V3** ★★ Start on #20 and finish on Kevin's Traverse.

❏ **22. Kevin's Traverse V0** ★★ Start on the lowest part of the rail. Traverse right using the low boulder to a finish at the apex of the boulder to the right.

❏ **23. Project** Start low with a large squeeze. Climb straight up.

❏ **24. Unnamed V2** ★★ ! Climb the left-leaning arête to a finish just left of the apex.

❏ **25. Unnamed V4** ★ Sit start with opposing edges. Climb right on the slopey angled shelf.

❏ **26. The First Glasses V8** ★★ Sit start on the left side of the bulge with a right hand crimp and a left hand sidepull. Make a move right and then bear hug your way out the prow.

Joe's Garage

❏ **27. Unnamed V0** ★ Climb the slab.

❏ **28. Joe's Garage V5** ★★ Start on the left side and climb under the roof and out the other side.

❏ **29. The Mechanic V6** ★★ Sit start to the right. Climb leftwards and then up.

The Zorro Boulder

❏ **30. Unnamed V0-** ★★ Climb the rail just right of the tree from a high start.

❏ **31. Project** Climb straight up the face from slopers.

❏ **32. Zorro V4** ★★★ Start on a shoulder-height sloper. Go right to the flake and then make a big move straight up. (V2 from a high start on the flake).

❏ **33. Unnamed V5** ★★ Start with a left hand undercling and a right hand pinch. Climb straight up just left of the tree.

❏ **34. Unnamed V0** ★ Climb the flakes just right of the tree.

❏ **35. Project** Start low with right-facing holds. Climb up through slopers to the topout.

New Deli Boulder

❏ **36. Unnamed VB** ★ Start with your right hand on the angled arête. Stand up on the slab and then reach the shelf.

❏ **37. Unnamed V0** ★ Start on the right side of the arête and climb around it left to the shelf.

❏ **38. New Deli Line V0** ★★ With your left hand on an undercling, jump to the good holds high above. Continue straight up.

❏ **39. New Delhi Freight Train V4** ★★ Start on two right-facing sidepulls. Dyno to the lip and then mantel.

❏ **40. Unnamed V1** ★ Climb the left side of the arête from a sit start.

❏ **41. Rail Runner VB** ★★ Climb the arête from a stand start on the left side.

❏ **42. Unnamed V3** ★ Start sitting with crimps. Go up and left to the arête.

❏ **43. Unnamed V4** ★ Start sitting with crimps and climb right to the jug at the white dike. Then finish straight up
.

❏ **44. Unnamed VB** ★★ Start on the jug at the white dike and climb straight up.

❏ **45. Unnamed VB** ★ Climb the face.

❏ **46. Unnamed VB** ★ Climb the right side of the slab.

❏ **47. Unnamed V0** ★ Climb the face to a mantel.

❏ **48. Unnamed VB** ★ Climb the right side of the arête.

❏ **49. Unnamed VB** ★ Climb the left side of the arête.

❏ **50. Unnamed V3** ★★ Climb the center of the slab.

❏ **51. Unnamed VB** ★ Climb the arête.

Happy Isles

Approach time: **25-30 minutes**

Number of problems: **1**

There are several clusters of boulders in the vicinity of Happy Isles (the trailhead from Half Dome). However, not much has been developed in this area. There are many boulders along the well-traveled first section of the Mist Trail. Additionally, you will find boulders lining the horse trail past (north of) the Happy Isles bridge.

Cedar Eater

This classic roof offwidth is located on the right (south) side of the Mist Trail. Hike for about 3⁄4 miles past the trailhead. Eventually you will come to a rock wall that lines the right side of the trail. At the end of this wall, the trail dips and there is a steep, short, mossy rock face on the left. Bushwhack down and left to the river at this point. The Cedar Eater is under a boulder right next to the river. There are several other established problems in this area.

❏ **1. Cedar Eater V5 ★★★★** Start on the east end of the roof near a sharp rock. Climb the roof and exit into the corner near the river. This burly problem will probably require you to invent a few new techniques.

Randy Puro on Drive On (V10). Photo by Tim Medina.

Horse Trail

Approach time: **5-15 minutes**

Number of problems: **27**

There are many boulders scattered around the Horse Trail east of the Ahwahnee Hotel. A few little areas are described here but there is potential for many more problems in this region. There are also many boulders along the horse trail beyond the Indian Caves. The areas are listed in the order you would encounter them if hiking from the Ahwahnee Hotel.

Approach

Park at the Ahwahnee Hotel and join the horse trail next to the parking lot and entrance road (see Ahwahnee Boulders topo). Follow this trail east towards Tenaya Canyon. The first cluster of boulders is about a five-minute walk from the hotel. For all but the Great White area, it is shorter to follow the gated dirt road at the northeast end of the parking lot. This road/wide trail leads to a bike path and a bridge. Go left on the bike path and join the horse trail when it comes close to the bike path. These areas can also be approached from the Stables.

Paul Barraza on Drive On (V10). Photo by Noah Kaufman

The Great White Area

These two problems are on a boulder that sits next to the right side of the horse trail about four minutes from the Ahwahnee Hotel. The problems face the trail.

❏ **1. Unnamed V2** ★ Reach high edges on the left side of the face and climb up and right.

❏ **2. Great White V1** ★★★ Start on high angled slopers. Climb left to holds and then up and right to the top.

Number of problems by difficulty

VB	V0	V1	V2	V3	V4	V5	V6	V7	V8	V9	V10	≥V11
6	4	3	2	3	1	0	0	1	2	2	2	0

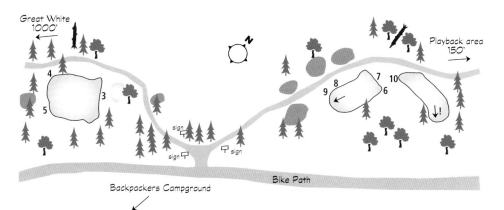

The Kauk Face Area

This area lies next to the bike path and is distinguished by a division in the trail with three trail signs.

❏ **3. Unnamed VB** ★ Climb angled jugs.

❏ **4. Unnamed VB** ★ Climb rounded jugs on the faint arête left of the trees.

❏ **5. Unnamed V0-** ★★ ! Climb the corner just left of the arête.

❏ **6. Project** Climb the left arête.

❏ **7. Kauk Face V8** ★★ ! Climb straight up the face from a high angled hold in a rock scar. This was originally a TR but has probably been bouldered.

❏ **8. Unnamed V4** ★ Start with right-facing sidepulls. Climb straight up.

❏ **9. Unnamed V0-** ★ Climb the right arête.

❏ **10. Unnamed V2** ★ Climb the arête.

The Playback Area

This area is just past the Kauk Face Area.

☐ **11. Playback VB ★** ! Climb the mossy angled jugs right of the arête. The upper part of this problem is dirty so it may be better to downclimb the problem.

☐ **12. Unnamed V3 ★** Sit start the arête. Go right to a mantel at the left-facing feature.

☐ **13. Unnamed V3 ★** Start with a head-height right hand edge and a higher left hand sloper. Climb straight up.

☐ **14. Unnamed V0 ★★** Start with edges 6 ft. left of the arête. Go straight up to a jug above the lip.

☐ **15. Unnamed VB ★** Start with a protruding fin jug. Climb the right side of the arête.

☐ **16. Unnamed V1 ★** Start with a head-height edge and go straight up to a jug.

The Mini-Meanies

This boulder is about 30 ft. left of the horse trail shortly before the Indian Caves. The crack faces the trail. (See photo).

☐ **17. Unnamed V9 ★★** Squeeze both arêtes of the leaning rock.

☐ **18. Left Mini-Meanie V0 ★★** Climb the wider left crack.

☐ **19. Right Mini-Mini V1 ★★** Climb the right crack. Ring locks to handjams.

☐ **20. Half Pint V7 ★★** ! Climb the leaning tips crack. This is often toproped.

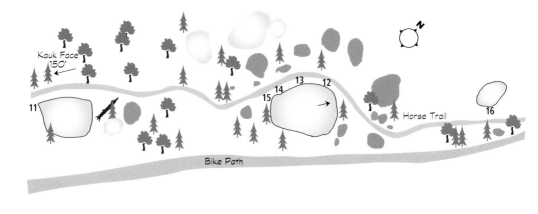

The Indian Caves

This area includes some classic hard problems. The caves here are also fun to explore. These are the big boulders in a clearing with hanging wires. Drive On is visible from the trail. (See section photo).

❏ **21. Drive On** V10 ★★★★ !
Start on a high good edge near the left side of the face. Make a big move right to smaller edges and then climb up and slightly left.

❏ **22. Unnamed** V3 ★ Climb either side of the arête that is left (north) of the chimney.

❏ **23. Unnamed** VB ★★ ! Climb the chimney.

❏ **24. Triangle Man** V5 ★★
Climb the arête right of the chimney from a sit start.

❏ **25. Ghost Rider** V10 ★★ Climb the right side of the left arête from a stand start.

❏ **26. Little Blue Anasthesia** V8 ★★ Climb the right arête (the left side of the chimney) from a stand start.

❏ **27. Unnamed** VB ★★ ! Climb the chimney.

❏ **28. The Misfit** V9 ★★ Climb the arête right of the chimney from a stand start.

Ahwahnee Boulders - East

Approach time: **1 minute**

Number of problems: **24**

This is a great circuit of problems somewhat off the beaten path – though definitely near a beaten path. Most of the boulders here are smaller and sport good problems for those afraid of highballs. A few cool air pockets make this area slightly cooler in the warmer months.

Approach

Drive or take the bus to the Ahwahnee Hotel. The Boulders line the horse trail that parallels the entrance road and the parking areas.

This sector starts at the biggest boulder near the parking lot and extends east to where the horse trail curves uphill.

❏ **1. Project** Start standing with good edges and climb the thin concave face.

❏ **2. Ketchup Machine V4** ★ ! Start the same as Hamburger Helper. Move left to edges halfway up the face and top out to the left.

❏ **3. Hamburger Helper V3** ★★ ! Start sitting with the big rail. Climb straight up the face.

❏ **4. Silly Roof V7** ★★ Start on jugs deep under the roof. Climb out the roof and mantel slightly to the left on the sloping lip.

The Ahwahnee Boulder

❏ **5. Unnamed V3** ★ ! Start low on the left arête. Traverse up and right on sloping holds to jugs.

❏ **6. Cilley V10** ★ Climb up and slightly right on sidepulls and sharp crimps.

❏ **7. Pugelist V9** ★★ Start sitting with positive crimps. Climb up the steep prow to the face to the right.

❏ **8. Sun Salutation V5** ★ Start standing right of the Pugelist. Climb up and slightly left to join the finish of Pugelist.

❏ **9. Ahwahnee Arête V4** ★★★ ! Start standing at the rounded arête and climb straight up using slopey sidepulls. Finish with scary slab moves.

❏ **10. Project** Climb up the center of the face with slopey dishes.

❏ **11. Unnamed V2** ★★ ! Start on undercling and climb straight up the arête.

Number of problems by difficulty

VB	V0	V1	V2	V3	V4	V5	V6	V7	V8	V9	V10	≥V11
3	1	1	2	5	2	1	1	2	2	3	1	0

❏ **12. Unnamed VB** ★ ! Climb the slab.

❏ **13. Unnamed V0-** ★ Start sitting and pull up the face.

❏ **14. Unnamed V3** ★★ Start sitting at the right end of the sloping rail. Traverse up and left to a mantel at an incut shelf.

❏ **15. Unnamed VB** ★ Mantel at the incut shelf.

❏ **16. Five Happiness V1** ★★ Start on high slopey jugs and climb up the arête.

❏ **17. Cryptochild V9** Start under the low roof and pull over the bulge.

❏ **18. Project** Start on the left side and traverse right on the lip over a bad landing.

❏ **19. On The Return V2** ★ ! Start high on the right arête. Climb up and left to a mantel near the top of the arête.

❏ **20. Front Seat V8** ★★ Start on the big rail and dyno to a sloper at the lip.

❏ **21. T-rex V3** ★ Start on a low diagonal rail. Crank to the jug and then to the top.

❏ **22. Unnamed V6** ★ Climb the slab 8 ft. left of the right end of the boulder. Start standing.

❏ **23. Unnamed VB** ★ Climb the arête above the angled shelf.

❏ **24. Unnamed V7** ★★ Start under the roof at the lower boulder. Move out to the lip holds and then crank straight up to the top.

❏ **25. Pommel Horse V8** ★★ Start on #24 and climb rightwards and up at the lip.

❏ **26. Project** Climb the face just left of the arête from a low start.

❏ **27. Pressure Drop V9** ★★ ! Jump the big angled sloper above the lip. Mantel this and climb to the top.

❏ **28. Project** Climb the steep cave to a blank face.

❏ **29. Growing Stone V3** ★ Start on high slopers right of the arête. Go straight up using the arête. Boulder A

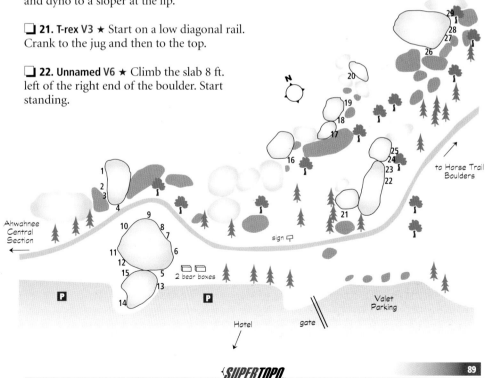

Approach time: **10 seconds**

Number of problems: **31**

❏ **1. Project** Climb the Bulldog Problem and then continue left along the low lip to a mantel at the end.

❏ **2. The Bulldog Problem V3** ★ Start sitting with slopey holds. Move up to the obvious sidepull and then finish to the left.

❏ **3. Project** Climb the face with gastons and sidepulls.

❏ **4. Unnamed V1** Climb the left arête from a jug start.

❏ **5. Unnamed VB** ★ Climb the arête left of the tree.

❏ **6. Blonde Ambition V6** ★★ Start on Smile for the Green Dragon and continue left along the lip to a slopey mantel.

❏ **7. Smile For the Green Dragon V5** ★★ Start sitting with your right hand on the arête and your left hand on the low rail. Dyno up and mantel to the right.

❏ **8. Atlas V5** ★★ Start on the jug and dyno to the lip using the sidepull if it helps.

❏ **9. Men From Mars V2** ★ Start on the left side of the boulder with good holds. Traverse rightwards along the lip.

❏ **10. Women from Venus V3** ★ Start low on the sloping diagonal rail. Dyno up and then mantel.

Lisa Davidson on #28 (V0).
Photo by Matt Wilder.

❏ **11. Syndrome V3** ★ Start sitting with a jug and a crimp. Move up the arête to a slab finish.

❏ **12. Project** Traverse leftwards along the boulder to a finish at the point.

❏ **13. Across the Abyss V2** ★ ! Step over the gap to grab opposing sidepulls and then move to the top.

❏ **12. Unnamed V0** ★ Start on a low big flat edge and go straight up.

Number of problems by difficulty

VB	V0	V1	V2	V3	V4	V5	V6	V7	V8	V9	V10	≥V11
2	3	3	2	7	0	5	5	2	1	1	1	0

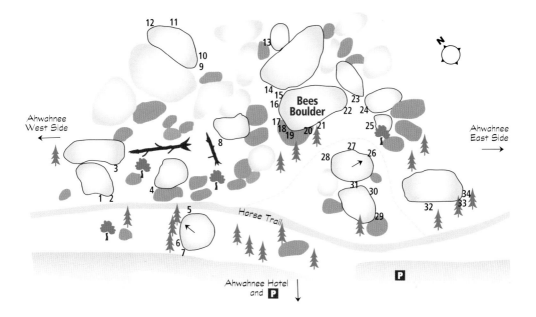

The Bees Boulder

❏ **15. Sports Action Direct V6** ★ Start low with one hand on each side of the arête. Move up to the sloping rail and then continue to the top.

❏ **16. Sports Action V7** ★ Start with crimps on the face. Go to the slopey rail and then to the slopey dish. Finish to the right.

❏ **17. Unnamed V1** Start on Juice Man and go straight up.

❏ **18. Juice Man V5** ★ Start sitting with the left vertical slot. Traverse right all the way to the finish of Beached Whale.

❏ **19. Unnamed V1** Start with the rail and go up and left.

❏ **20. Squeeze V5** ★ Start standing with sloping holds and bad feet. Move up right to a good crimp and then traverse right to the Beached Whale mantel.

❏ **21. Joss V7** ★ Start with crimps on the overhanging face. Climb up and slightly left over the bulge.

❏ **22. Beached Whale V5** ★★ Start sitting at right side of boulder. Traverse left to a mantel just left of the fin.

❏ **23. Silent Spotter V6** ★★ ! Start standing. Climb up and left using the arête and face holds. Variation: Thong Cave V10 ** sit start to the left and climb up and right.

❏ **24. Dirty Dave** VB Climb the mossy face.

❏ **25. Munchkin Lunge** V6 ★ Start sitting with a crimp and a sidepull. Dyno to the top.

❏ **26. Unnamed** V0 Start standing at the right leaning dihedral and go straight up.

❏ **27. No Fur** V3 ★★ Climb straight up the slopey holds from a sit start.

❏ **28. Unnamed** V0 ★★ Climb the arête from a stand start.

❏ **29. Unnamed** V6 ★ Traverse right along the sloping lip.

❏ **30. Chokin'** V5 ★ Start standing with a pinch and a crimp. Go straight up. (Var: jump start V0).

❏ **31. Funky Chicken** V9 ★★ Start sitting, in between the boulders, with two slopey holds below a right-facing feature. Climb leftwards along the steep lip to join Chokin'.

❏ **32. Unnamed** V3 ★ Climb the right arête from a sit start.

❏ **33. Myles Traverse** V8 ★★ Traverse boulder from right to left.

❏ **34. Unnamed** V3 ★ Climb the first half of the Myles Traverse and then mantel in the middle of the boulder.

Lisa Davidson on No Fur (V3). Photo by Matt Wilder.

Ahwahnee Boulders - West

Approach time: 2 minutes

Number of problems: 29

These boulders are north of the entrance road just before the parking lots.

The first three problems are not on the topo, they are on one boulder west of the main boulders. The second two problems face the trail (see photo).

❏ **1. Unnamed V0** ★★ Climb the face starting with quartz edges at 6 ft.

❏ **2. 2X2 V6** ★ Climb the arête from a sit start.

❏ **3. 4X4 V8** ★★ Climb the center of the face from nearly a sit start. (V4 from stand).

❏ **4. Crazy Horse V9** ★★ ! Start at the lip with a sloper near a white dike. Go right to and angled edge and then straight up.

❏ **5. Project** Climb the steep face with a slab behind it from a stand start.

❏ **6. Downward Dog V7** ★ Start on slopers at the point and climb up and right.

❏ **7. Tweety Bird V7** ★ Start in the horizontal crack. Climb straight up into the end of Downward Dog.

❏ **8. Big Bird V8** ★ Climb the right side of the face.

❏ **9. Chimera V12** ★★ Start on an angled jug under a horizontal roof. Climb out the roof and then finish right after the lip.

❏ **10. Unnamed V8** ★ ! Climb the left-facing rail from a sit start.

Number of problems by difficulty

VB	V0	V1	V2	V3	V4	V5	V6	V7	V8	V9	V10	≥V11
1	4	1	2	2	3	3	2	3	3	3	0	2

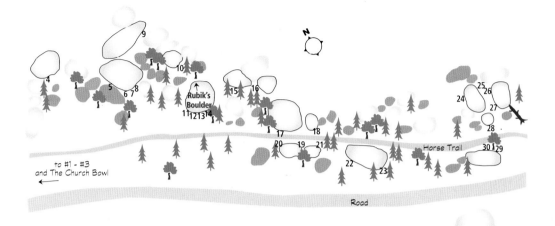

Rubik's Boulder

11. Unnamed V4 ★★ Climb the left arête from a stand start.

12. Unnamed V9 ★ Sit start in the middle of the wall and climb left to join #11.

13. Montezuma's Revenge V9 ★★★ Sit start in the middle of the face, climb into Rubik's Revenge, and then climb leftwards along the lip to the apex.

14. Rubik's Revenge V7 ★★ Start on a high right-facing hold and climb up and slightly right.

15. William "The Refrigerator" Perry V3 ★ Start on a jug and go right along the lip to another jug. Finish straight up.

16. The Dark Crystal V? ★ Start on a low incut. Climb up and right through the face to better crimps. Finish straight up.

17. Unnamed V0- ★★ Climb the left angling feature.

18. Unnamed VB ★ Climb the arête.

19. Training Bra V4 ★ Start low on two slopey holds next to each other.

20. The Fridge V5 ★★ Start sitting on right side of boulder. Traverse the two obvious incut rails. Mantel out left after the second rail.

21. Mellow Yellow V1 ★ Dyno from jugs to top. The bottom is off.

22. Birk Crack V2 Layback the short crack from a sit start.

23. Low Rail V0 ★ Climb the face with a low rail.

24. Stacked V3 ★ Sit start and climb straight up.

25. Extreme Marine V5 ★★ ! Start standing to the left. Move right up the rail to a jug. Then move back left to the top of fin.

26. Pump'n Live V2 ★ Sit start in the slot. Climb up the arête using both sides.

27. Denominator V6 ★★ Start with your left hand on an undercling and your right hand on the lip. Do a hard move up and right and then mantel slightly to left. (Variation project: sit start).

28. Dave's Proud Mantel V0 ★ Start sitting. Mantel into low scoop.

29. Dead Precedence V5 ★★ Start on the face with a left hand low sidepull and a right hand high sidepull. Go out left to the arête and then up.

30. Go Go Gorilla V4 ★★ Start on big high edge on the face and climb straight up.

Sasha Musso on Camp 4 West #41 (VB). Photo by Matt Wilder.

Indian Creek

Approach time: **5-15 minutes**

Number of problems: **37**

Indian Creek.

This area sports a few classic problems in a location that sees little traffic. The gem of the area is definitely the Medicine Man Boulder. This tall rock has some great featured vertical problems and perhaps some potential for new tall highballs and harder problems. During the spring, the creek runs in full force adding, nicely to the ambiance. During the late summer and fall, the creek is sometimes dry.

Approach

Parking for this area is at the Church Bowl. If you follow signs to the Ahwahnee Hotel, you will drive past the Village Store parking lot and then turn right. On your left, after the turn, is the medical and dental clinic. The Church Bowl is just beyond the clinic on the left; you will see picnic tables and a cliff close to the road. To get to the boulders, follow the trail that leads up from the left (west) side of the parking pullout.

Number of problems by difficulty

VB	V0	V1	V2	V3	V4	V5	V6	V7	V8	V9	V10	≥V11
10	14	5	2	2	0	1	1	0	0	0	0	0

Free Clinic Boulder

This lone boulder is on the right side of the trail about 600 ft. from the parking area. It comes just before a residence that is on the left side of the trail.

❑ **1. The Cool Long Warm-up VB** ★★ ! Climb the obtuse corner from a high start.

❑ **2. Unnamed V0** ★★ Follow seams up the arête.

❑ **3. Unnamed V0** ★ Climb right of the arête above a low roof.

❑ **4. Unnamed V0** ★★ Start on high holds left of the moss. Rock over a good foot shelf and then finish straight up.

❑ **5. Unnamed V6** ★ Start from a low right-facing sidepull. Make a big move left to a crimp rail and then go straight up.

❑ **6. Unnamed V1** ★ Start on a high jug left of where the two boulders meet. Go up and slightly right.

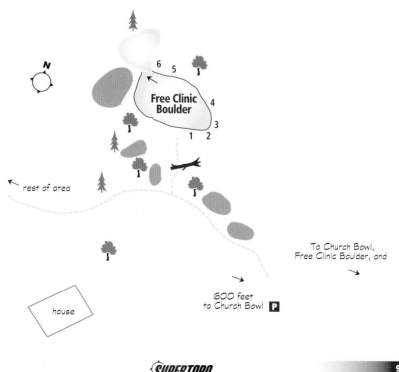

Indian Creek - East Side

These boulders lie on the east side of Indian Creek. When hiking from the Church Bowl parking, head right just before the bridge that crosses the creek. Follow the creek uphill until it jags to the left. The first boulders will be on your right at this point.

The Powwow Boulder

☐ **1. Project** Start standing with the arête and a crimp on the face. Traverse up and right on the sloping rail.

☐ **2. The Scalpel V3** ★ Climb the center of the face from a high start.

☐ **3. Jug of Whine V3** ★★ Start on the high angled jug. Climb straight up.

☐ **4. Unnamed V2** ★ Start on the right side of the face and traverse left along the lip.

☐ **5. Unnamed V0** ★ Mantel the high jug.

☐ **6. Unnamed V0** ★ Sit start with a jug at the right side of the boulder. Climb straight up using the arête.

☐ **7. Cardiac Arête V0** ★★ Climb the prow from a high start on small edges. (Low start from opposing crimps is V3).

☐ **8. Unnamed V0** ★ Climb the scoopy slab.

☐ **9. Unnamed V0** ★ Climb the left arête.

☐ **10. Unnamed V1** ★ Climb the white dike from a start on head-height edges.

☐ **11. Unnamed V0** ★ Climb the right arête.

☐ **12. Project** Climb the features behind the trees.

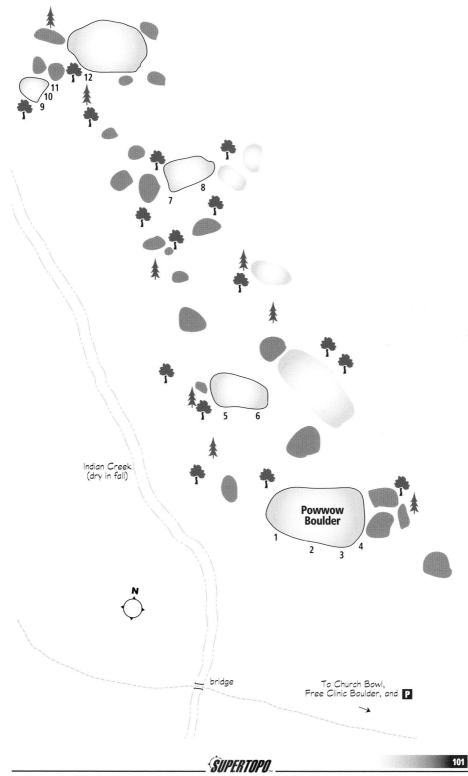

Indian Creek
(dry in fall)

**Powwow
Boulder**

To Church Bowl,
Free Clinic Boulder, and ▣

bridge

N

Indian Creek - West Side

To find this area, hike for a few minutes past the bridge that crosses Indian Creek. You will see some bigger boulders on your right about 150 ft. past a switchback. Head straight uphill just after these boulders. After about 400 ft. of uphill hiking, you will run into the Medicine Man Boulder.

Intern Boulder

❑ **1. Unnamed VB** ★ Climb the juggy face.

❑ **2. Unnamed VB** ★ Climb the arête.

❑ **3. Unnamed VB** ★★ Climb the center of the face.

❑ **4. Unnamed VB** ★ Climb the right side of the face.

❑ **5. Unnamed V0** ★ Climb just left of the arête.

❑ **6. The Intern V0** ★★ Climb the line of jugs just right of the arête.

❑ **7. Unnamed VB** ★ Climb the juggy middle of the face.

Medicine Man Boulder

❑ **8. Unnamed VB** ! This dirty ramp is the descent. Make sure it is dry before you climb this boulder.

❑ **9. Double Decker V2** ★★★ ! Climb the right-facing corner from a head-height start.

❑ **10. Unnamed V0** ★★ ! Start with high edges and a sidepull. Climb straight up following a faint seam.

❑ **11. Unnamed V0** ★★ ! Start on edges at 5 ft. just left of a low, small right-facing corner. Climb straight up.

❑ **12. Unnamed V2** ★ ! Jump start to a slopey shelf on the arête. Mantel and then finish straight up.

❑ **13. Dr. Decker V1** ★ ! From the boulder at the base, reach across and mantel the shelf. Traverse left to the shallow hole and then finish straight up.

❑ **14. Unnamed V1** ★ ! Start on Dr. Decker and climb straight up from the shelf.

❑ **15. Project** Climb the very high "jug" haul.

❑ **16. Leo the Flathead VB** Traverse the low lip of the boulder opposite the descent for the Medicine Man Boulder. Go from right to left.

Matterhorn Boulder

❏ **17. Unnamed V0+** ★ Start high from the natural cheater stone just right of the tree. Go straight up.

❏ **18. Unnamed VB** ★★ Climb the arête.

❏ **19. The Matterhorn VB** ★★ Reach high to the jug 4 ft. right of the arête and go up and right.

❏ **20. Unnamed V5** ★★ Start with a left hand crimp and a right hand sidepull at head height. Climb straight up past the right-facing feature.

Gravitational Pull Boulder

❏ **21. Unnamed V0-** ★ Climb edges up the left side of the face from a high start.

❏ **22. Unnamed V1** ★ Start in the 'V' and traverse left to finish on #21.

❏ **23. Project** Start at ground level with the angled crack. Go up and right to the top. This will be a classic highball if it is cleaned well.

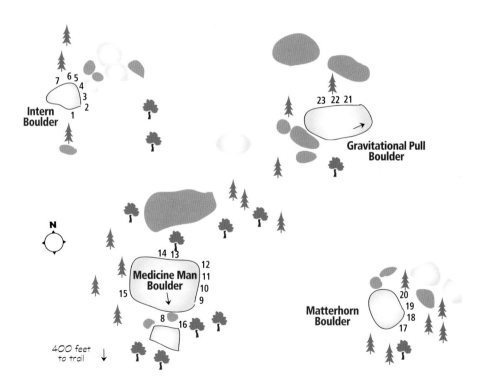

Lower Yosemite Falls

Approach time: **5 minutes**

Number of problems: **27**

These boulders line the paved trail that leads to Lower Yosemite Falls. There are a few fun problems here, but you will not find any solitude here. The gem of the area is definitely Park Life, a hard, technical corner past the falls.

Approach

Park in the Yosemite Lodge parking lot and hike across the road to catch the Lower Yosemite Falls trail. The main area is on the left side of the trail.

Plaque Boulder

This boulder is on the left side of the trail 80 ft. before the trail splits. It is not on the topo.

❏ **1. Unnamed** V0 ★ Climb the slab facing the trail.

❏ **2. Unnamed** VB ★ Climb the right arête of the face that does not face the trail.

❏ **3. Mini-Stein-Way** V3 ★★ Climb the splitter from a sit start.

❏ **4. Falk's Fracture** V2 ★★ Sit start low in the crack. Climb straight out.

❏ **5. Falk's Fracture Traverse** V2 ★★ Climb Falk's Fracture and then traverse to a mantel at the right end.

❏ **6. Unnamed** V0+ ★★ Start at the right end and traverse left to finish on Falk's Fracture.

❏ **7. Unnamed** V0 ★ Climb the arête next to the tree.

❏ **8. Unnamed** V0 ★ Climb the face from a high start.

Number of problems by difficulty

VB	V0	V1	V2	V3	V4	V5	V6	V7	V8	V9	V10	≥V11
5	8	4	6	2	0	0	1	0	0	0	0	1

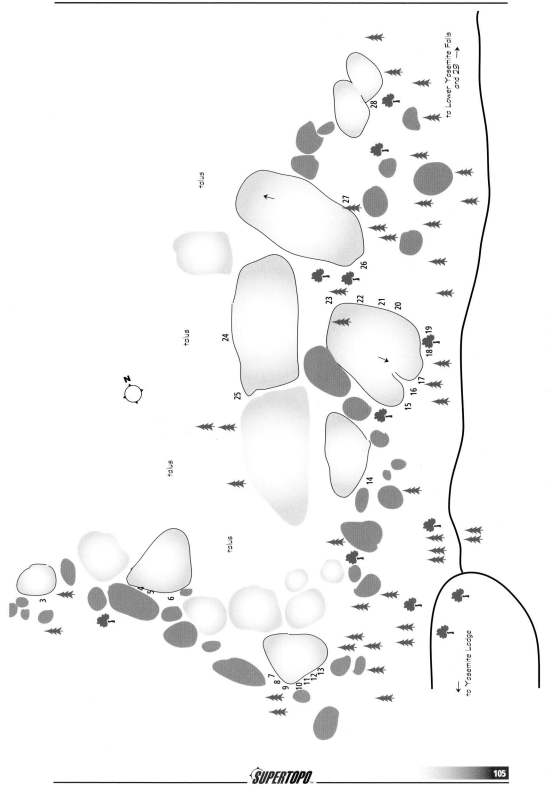

❏ **9. Unnamed V0+** ★ Climb the left side of the arête.

❏ **10. Unnamed VB** ★★ ! Climb the face just right of the arête.

❏ **11. Unnamed VB** ★★ ! Start on a high shelf and follow the seam to the top.

❏ **12. Unnamed V1** ★ ! Climb the face just left of the left-facing feature.

❏ **13. Unnamed V2** ★★ Climb the left-facing corner.

❏ **14. Unnamed VB** ★ Hand traverse the low flat boulder in either direction.

❏ **15. Unnamed V1** ★★ Climb the mossy right-facing corner that leads to a seam.

❏ **16. Unnamed VB** ★ Climb the chimney.

❏ **17. Unnamed V2** ★★ Climb the arête on the right side of the chimney.

❏ **18. 5150 V2** ★ Jam deep in the awkward flare.

❏ **19. Unnamed V0** ★ Climb the face 4 ft. right of the tree from a high sidepull.

❏ **20. Unnamed V2** ★★ ! Start at a head-height crimp 4 ft. left of the main fissure. Climb up and then right to join #21.

❏ **21. Unnamed V0** ★★ ! Climb the main fissure.

❏ **22. Unnamed V0** ★★ ! Climb the face to the shelf and then to the juggy lip.

❏ **23. Unnamed V3** ★★ ! Climb the right side of the arête using the seam to the right. Stand start.

❏ **24. Project** Climb the flakes to a bulge and then to a high topout.

❏ **25. Project** Climb the high sharp arête.

❏ **26. Pop Top V6** ★★ ! Start on the jug, go left and then up to the shelf. Down climb the tree or continue up the tree.

❏ **27. Unnamed V1** ★ ! Climb the slab.

❏ **28. Unnamed V1** ★ ! Climb the offwidth between the two corners. Seasonally wet.

29. Park Life V12 ★★★ To get to this problem, follow the trail past the bridge that crosses the Falls river. Continue on this trail until it leads into a boulder. A platform is built around the boulder for the trail. At the start of the platform, grab an undercling and a sidepull. Climb the left-facing corner. This problem is best done in the off season to avoid the crowds. Don't block the trail with pads.

Yosemite Falls.

Swan Slab

Approach time: **3 minutes**

Number of problems: **25**

This Swan Slab is probably the most popular climbing area in the Valley. The boulders here are less crowded and offer some fun problems.

Approach

From the Camp 4 parking lot, follow a trail northeast towards Yosemite Falls. The boulders will be on your left before you reach the Swan Slab climbing area.

Bridwell Boulder

❏ **1. Unnamed V0** ★ Climb the arête past a seam. Sit start with a right-facing jug.

❏ **2. Unnamed V0-** ★ Climb the left-angling faint arête.

❏ **3. Unnamed V1** ★ Climb rightwards into the Ducktail Mantel from a sit start.

❏ **4. Ducktail Mantel V0-** ★ Mantel the left side of the shelf.

❏ **5. Pitter-Patter Traverse V1** ★ Start at the right side of the lip and traverse left to finish on the Ducktail Mantel.

❏ **6. Unnamed V3** ★ Mantel the right side of the lip without using the good features to the right.

❏ **7. Unnamed VB** ★ Climb the right-facing feature.

❏ **8. Unnamed VB** ★ Climb the face above two angled crimps.

❏ **9. Unnamed V0-** ★★ Climb just right of the main black streak.

❏ **10. Unnamed V4** ★★ Climb the arête from a sit start.

❏ **11. Unnamed V0-** ★ Reach a high hold on the face next to a seam and climb straight up.

Number of problems by difficulty

VB	V0	V1	V2	V3	V4	V5	V6	V7	V8	V9	V10	≥V11
8	7	2	1	5	2	0	0	0	0	0	0	0

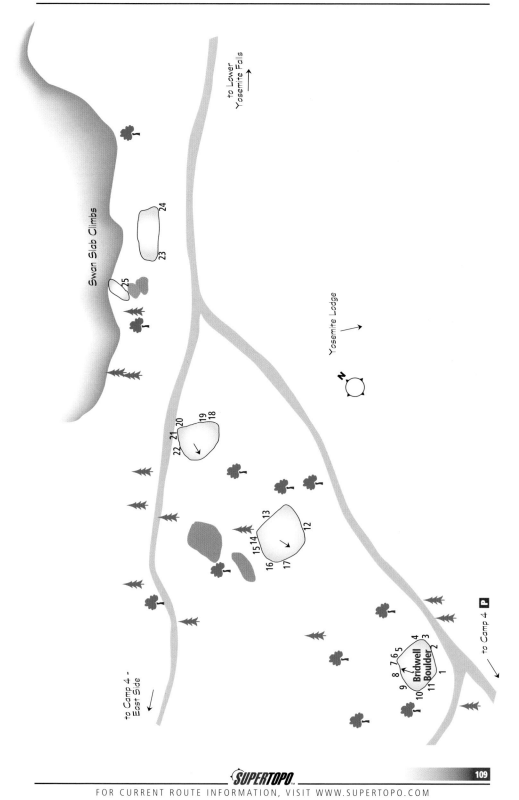

Swan Slab Climbs

to Lower
Yosemite Falls

Yosemite Lodge

N

to Camp 4 -
East Side

to Camp 4

Bridwell
Boulder

❏ **12. I'm Pumped** V3 ★★ Reach the juggy lip and traverse around the corner.

❏ **13. Unnamed** V4 ★ Start on low polished crimps. Climb up and slightly right.

❏ **14. Unnamed** VB ★★ Climb the right-facing feature.

❏ **15. Unnamed** VB ★ Climb the face above a flake jug.

❏ **16. Unnamed** VB ★ Climb the arête.

❏ **17. Unnamed** VB ★★ Climb the right-facing feature.

❏ **18. The Sloth Left** V2 ★ Start on The Sloth and climb up and left to a mantel.

❏ **19. The Sloth** V3 ★ Sit start at the angled rail and traverse right around the corner to an easy mantel.

❏ **20. Unnamed** V3 ★ Climb the right arête from a sit start.

❏ **21. Unnamed** VB ★★ Climb right of the arête on an undercling lieback. Start high.

❏ **22. Unnamed** VB ★ Climb the face from a high start.

❏ **23. Lazy Sloth** V0- ★ Traverse the lip left to right. Mantel at the end.

❏ **24. California Edge** V3 ★ Sit start and climb the left-angling arête.

❏ **25. Unnamed** V0 ★★ Climb the arête starting high near the left boulder. Mantel just before the right boulder.

Olivier Plante on Cocaine Corner (V5). Photo by Matt Wilder.

Camp 4 - Overview

Approach time: **2 minutes**

Number of problems: **219**

This is the highest concentrated bouldering area in the Valley. It is home to the mega-classics such as Bachar Cracker, Midnight Lightning, King Cobra, Thriller and the Dominator. Camp 4 is also the historic campground where climbers have lived for the past 60 years. The rock in Camp 4 has larger grains than some of the other granite in the Valley making some of the holds sharper. Because it has been the center of Valley bouldering for many years, lots of the classic problems sport polished holds and have become harder.

Approach

Park in the Camp 4 parking lot and walk into the campground. The boulders lie uphill from the campground.

Jason Kehl on The Moffit Start (V10). Photo by Matt Wilder.

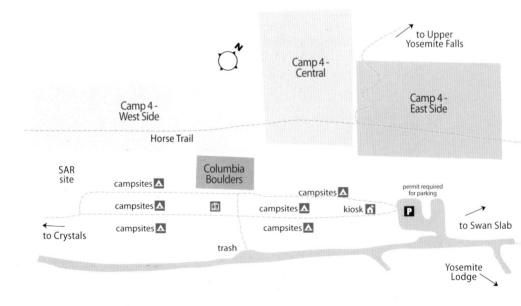

Camp 4 - Columbia Boulders

Approach time: **1 minute**

Number of problems: **18**

These are the quintessential Yosemite boulders located in the middle of Camp 4.

Big Columbia

To get off this boulder, downclimb the deciduous tree behind The Robbins Problem.

❏ **1. After Midnight V10 ★★** Start on Midnight Lightning and climb left and up through sidepulls and an ugly glued crimp.

❏ **2. Midnight Lightning V8 ★★★★** ! This could be the most famous boulder problem in the world and it deserves to be. Start with a head-height right hand crimp and a high left hand sidepull crimp. Climb up and right to the notorious mantel. First climbed by Ron Kauk in 1978, this problem revolutionized bouldering in America.

❏ **3. Kauk Start V9 ★** ! Start on high crimps directly below the mantel of Midnight Lightning. Climb straight up.

❏ **4. The Moffat Start V10 ★★★** ! Jump start to an angled sloper. Then traverse left to the mantel of Midnight Lightning.

❏ **5. Midnight Cowboy V9 ★** ! Start on crimps at the bottom of the left-facing corner. Go up and right to join #6.

❏ **6. The Robbins Problem V3 ★★** ! Start on the right-facing feature. Climb up and left to the left-facing feature. Finish straight up the scary mossy slab.

❏ **7. The Bates Problem V4 ★★★** ! Start on head-height holds at a six-inch roof. Climb straight up.

❏ **8. Unnamed V0 ★★★** ! Jump start to a jug and then climb up and left to a mantel at the point of the triangle.

❏ **9. Chouinard Mantel V1 ★★** ! Jump to the jug and mantel straight up.

❏ **10. Don't Make Me Kick Your Ass V9 ★★** Start standing with opposing sidepull crimps. Slap slopers up and left to finish on Chouinard Mantel.

❏ **11. End of the Day Problem V5 ★★** Sit start the arête and climb up and left to a tough mantel.

❏ **12. Unnamed V0 ★** ! The chipped slab.

Little Columbia Boulder

❏ **13. Unnamed V0 ★** Climb the left side of the arête above a flake at the base.

❏ **14. All Start Movie Mantel V1 ★** Mantel the high protruding point.

❏ **15. Unnamed VB ★** Climb straight up from slopey jugs.

❏ **16. Unnamed VB ★** Climb the left angling ramp.

❏ **17. Unnamed V0 ★** Climb the blunt arête starting with a left hand crimp.

❏ **18. Unnamed VB ★** Go up edges on the back face.

❏ **19. Unnamed V1 ★** Start on slopers at

Number of problems by difficulty

VB	V0	V1	V2	V3	V4	V5	V6	V7	V8	V9	V10	≥V11
3	4	2	0	1	1	1	0	0	1	3	2	0

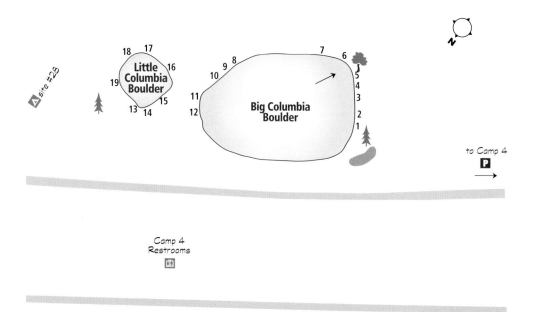

Camp 4 - East

Approach time: **4 minutes**

Number of problems: **49**

These boulders lie above the Camp 4 kiosk and east of the beginning of the Upper Yosemite Falls trail.

❏ **1. Unnamed V3** ★ Start with a right hand sidepull crimp. Go left and up.

❏ **2. The Shrink V3** ★★ Start with a head-height flake jug. Climb up and slightly right.

❏ **3. The Zschiesche Problem V3** ★ Climb the slab 6 ft. right of the left arête.

❏ **4. Smear Out V4** Climb the slab just right of The Zschiesche Problem.

❏ **5. The Glass Pyramid Face V1** ★★ ! Climb the face left of the right arête.

❏ **6. The Glass Pyramid Arête V0-** ★★ Climb the right arête.

Brittney Griffith on The Kor Problem (V3).
Photo by Dean Fidelman.

❏ **7. Unnamed VB** ★ Climb the arête above the big flake.

❏ **8. Unnamed V1** ★★ Traverse the face rightwards starting from the big face.

❏ **9. Unnamed V0** ★ Climb the left side of the right arête from a sit start.

❏ **10. Unnamed VB** ★ Climb the right side of the arête.

Number of problems by difficulty

VB	V0	V1	V2	V3	V4	V5	V6	V7	V8	V9	V10	≥V11
4	8	5	1	9	7	3	2	2	3	3	2	1

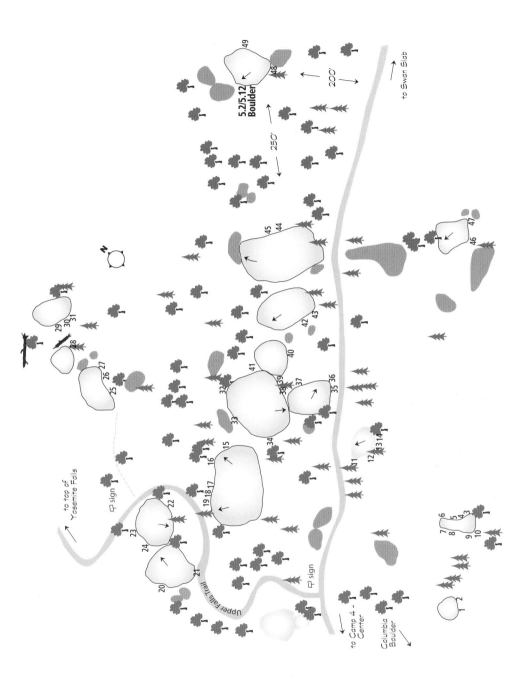

❏ **11. Unnamed V3** ★ Climb the arête from a sit start.

❏ **12. Kor Problem V3** ★★ ! Start standing just left of the tree. Climb up and left.

❏ **13. Klingon V5** ★★ Start right of the tree. Climb up the arête and then rightwards under the big flake. Finish straight up from the right side of the flake. (Var: this is slightly easier if you start left of the tree and traverse into the flake).

❏ **14. Kauk-a-holic V8** ★ Climb the face left of the tree from a high start.

❏ **15. The Largo Lunge V0-** ★★★ Climb the angling shelves from a stand start.

❏ **16. The Jimi Hendrix Experience V0** ★ ! Traverse the crack left to right. Start on a big jug and drop off on the right side.

❏ **17. Bachar Cracker V4** ★★★★ ! Sit start the crack with the flake jug. Climb straight out.

❏ **18. Unnamed V0** ★ Climb the finish of Bachar Cracker from the horizontal crack.

❏ **19. Unnamed V1** ★★ ! Traverse the crack right to left. Top out on the left side.

❏ **20. King Cobra V8** ★★★★ ! Start high with the sloping jug on the right side of the dihedral. Climb straight up to better holds at the top.

❏ **21. Woodward Arête V4** ★★ ! Climb the slabby arête closest to the trail.

❏ **22. Unnamed V4** ★ Climb the arête from a high start.

❏ **23. Unnamed V1** ★ Climb the arête from a stand start.

❏ **24. Clean and Jerk V8** ★ Climb the right arête from a high start.

❏ **25. Unnamed V4** ★★ Start on high edges and dyno to the lip.

❏ **26. Unnamed V1** ★ Climb the left-leaning shelf from a high start.

❏ **27. Unnamed V2** ★ Climb the right arête from a sit start.

❏ **28. Flame Thrower V5** ★ Squeeze up the left side of the arête.

❏ **29. Seat of the Pants V7** ★ Traverse leftwards on the rail. Start on the right side and top out on the left side.

❏ **30. Delicate Flower V6** ★★ ! Start on the right side of the rail and dyno to the holds above.

❏ **31. Honor Among Thieves V9**
★★★ Climb the arête from a sit start. The stand start is V7.

❏ **32. The Font Problem V6** ★★
Climb the bulge from a stand start. V7 from the sit start.

❏ **33. Unnamed V0** ★★ ! Jump to the left side of the shelf and mantel.

❏ **34. Scissors for Lefty V12** ★★
Sit start with a decent right-facing sidepull. Make hard compression moves up and left.

❏ **35. Unnamed V4** ★ Climb the face below the rock scar from a sit start with a good jug.

❏ **36. Unnamed VB** ★ Climb the right side of the face.

❏ **37. Unnamed V7** ★ Climb the faint arête from a stand start.

❏ **38. Swamp Thing V5** ★★ Climb the right angling seam.

❏ **39. Sex Factor X V9** ★★★ Start with a high right hand sidepull crimp. Climb up and right to an angled jug. Then continue up and back left.

❏ **40. Unnamed V3** ★ Start sitting at the right side of the low boulder and climb left to a mantel.

❏ **41. The Rebirthing V3** ★ Start on the side of the boulder away from the trail. Squeeze underneath where the two boulders pinch together. Exit on the trail side.

❏ **42. Unnamed VB** ★ Climb the face above the shelf.

❏ **43. Unnamed V3** ★★ Climb the slab left of the low shelf.

❑ **44. The Force V9** ★★★ ! Start on Thriller and follow the black streak up and left. Move left to better holds at the top of the black streak and then finish straight up. This problem was graded 8a (V11) when it was first done and was one of the hardest problems in the Valley. Some of the holds were glued to preserve the problem. Later one of the glued holds was pried off with a crowbar by someone who was against gluing. This ended up leaving a bigger hold than existed previously–this is the positive hold up and left from the start. With this hold and the use of the match hold on Thriller (which wasn't used on the FA) the problem is significantly easier. In its current state, without eliminating any holds, the problem is probably stiff V9. Because many people have done this version thinking they were doing the V11, this new way has been nicknamed The Farce.

❑ **45. Thriller V10** ★★★★ ! This is probably one of the best problems in the world. Start on high crimps in the middle of the face and climb up and right. The positive hold up and left from the start did not exist on the first ascent (see The Force description). The addition of this hold does not change the difficulty of the problem.

❑ **46. Unnamed V0** ★★ Climb the left arête. Mantel the high shelf.

❑ **47. Yabo's Knife V4** ★★ ! Climb the right arête from a stand start.

❑ **48. Leroy V10** ★★ ! Start standing on the left side of the arête. Climb up and slightly right using the arête.

❑ **49. Unnamed V3** ★★ Climb the arête.

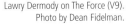

Paul Barraza on a Camp 4 project. Photo by Matt Wilder.

Lawry Dermody on The Force (V9).
Photo by Dean Fidelman.

Camp 4 - Center

Approach time: **3 minutes**

Number of problems: **64**

These boulders are directly above the first half of Camp 4 (between the kiosk and the bathrooms).

Arizona Avenue

❏ **1. Unnamed V3** ★★ Climb the left arête.

❏ **2. The Guerin Problem V4** ★★★ Climb the right side of the triangle starting with a high left hand gaston crimp and a right hand slopey sidepull.

❏ **3. Spanich Flies V3** ★ Start with the pointed feature at 5 ft. near the right side of the face. Climb up and right to the right-facing feature.

❏ **4. Aid Seminar V1** Climb the pin-scarred seam to the arête.

❏ **5. Pratt Mantel V0-** ★ Grab the good flake edge and climb straight up.

❏ **6. Bard's Flying Traverse Mantel V3** ★ Start on the Pratt Mantel and climb right to the arête and then up.

❏ **7. Back Stabber VB** ★ Climb the right side of the mossy face passing a right-facing feature.

❏ **8. Plastic Surgery V9** ★ Start on crimps at 7 ft. Go to the slopey lip and then mantel.

❏ **9. Unnamed VB** ★ Climb just left of the dead tree.

Courtney Hemphill on Sonic Wave (V8).
Photo by Tim Medina.

❏ **10. Unnamed VB** ★★ Climb the arête that faces away from the trail.

❏ **11. Unnamed V0** ★★ Start on a right-facing sidepull and climb straight up.

❏ **12. Unnamed V1** ★★ Start on big opposing sidepulls. Go up to the lip and then mantel.

❏ **13. Stinkbug V7** ★ Start 3 ft. left of the arête. Climb up the slab and then left along the lip.

❏ **14. Bugged V5** ★ Start on Stinkbug and climb straight up.

Number of problems by difficulty

VB	V0	V1	V2	V3	V4	V5	V6	V7	V8	V9	V10	≥V11
7	9	8	0	14	5	5	3	2	4	4	2	0

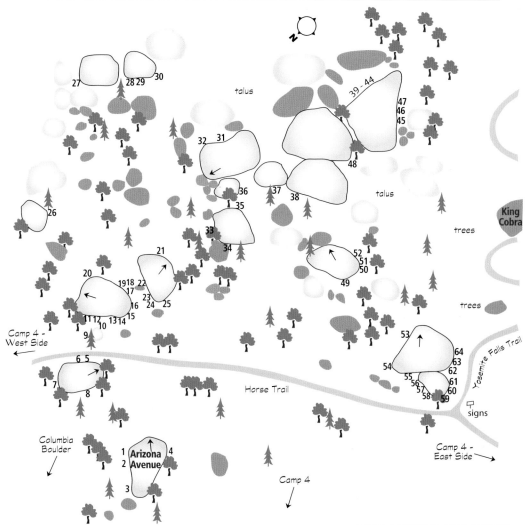

15. Higgins Problem V3 ★★
Climb the rounded arête / slab.

16. Hungry for More V6 ★ Start just right of the Higgins Problem and traverse the slopers right to finish on Blockhead.

17. Unnamed V5 ★ Start on Blockhead and climb up and left through slopers.

18. Blockhead V4 ★★ Climb the faint arête from a stand start.

19. Jump Head V3 ★ Jump start Blockhead.

20. Unnamed V1 ★★ Start on a shoulder-height sidepull jug and climb left along the lip / arête. (V0 if you use the block at the base).

21. The Sleeper V1 Start high on the black arête and climb straight up.

22. Unnamed V0- ★ ! Mantel at slopers into the right-facing corner.

23. Unnamed V1 ★ Mantel angled slopers.

24. Candy Ass V9 ★★ Start on #23 and traverse left to a mantel at the left side of the face.

25. Unnamed V0 ★ Climb the arête just left of the bush.

26. Sachmo V5 ★★ Start with a high right hand sidepull jug and a left hand sidepull sloper. Climb straight up.

27. Sonic Wave V8 ★★ Start standing with a left hand gaston and a right hand sidepull crimp flake. Climb up and slightly left.

28. Uncle Joe V3 ★★★ ! Start on high left-facing flat holds. Climb up and slightly right.

29. Killing Uncle Joe V6 ★ Start on Uncle Joe and traverse right on slopers to join the Webb Arête.

30. Webb Arête V3 ★★ Start right of the arête and climb up and left to finish on the arête.

31. Jackie Chan V10 ★★ Start standing at a left-facing feature and climb right into Bruce Lee.

32. Bruce Lee V8 ★★★ Climb the arête from a high start on the left side. There are a few hard variations that start right of the arête called Jet Li.

33. Unnamed V1 ★ Start on high angled crimps and climb straight up.

34. Bear-Hug Mantel V4 ★★ Start with opposing holds. Slap your way out to a mantel that is slightly to the right.

35. Lyn's Awesome Arête V3 ★ Start on high opposing holds with a horizontal seam between them. Climb straight up.

36. Unnamed V3 ★★ Sit start with crimps and climb up and right.

37. Glass House V3 ★★ Climb the face right of the arête from a stand start.

38. All Hands on Deck V8 ★★ Jump start to an angled slopey edge. Climb over the bulge.

Wills Young on Bruce Lee (V8). Photo by Dean Fidelman.

Energy Boulder

❏ **39. Fat Weasel V7** ★★ Climb the left-angling seam from a high start.

❏ **40. Hard Times V5** ★ Reach high crimps at the left side of the horizontal seam. Go straight up.

❏ **41. Unnamed V0** ★ Reach high to the best holds near the right side of the seam. Go up and right.

❏ **42. Unnamed V3** ★★ Reach the lip at its lowest point. Traverse left along the lip to the top of Fat Weasel.

❏ **43. Sharma Variation V10** ★★ Start on #44 and climb leftwards to join Fat Weasel. Stay below the lip.

❏ **44. Unnamed V1** ★★ Start on jugs above a pointed edge. Climb up and left to the top.

❏ **45. Oak Leaf Arête V3** ★ Climb the left arête.

❏ **46. Unnamed V5** ★★ Climb the slab 6 ft. right of the bottom of the arête.

❏ **47. Kumba** ★★★ ! Climb the slab at a low vertical white streak.

❏ **48. Well Preserved V9** ★★ Climb the arête left of the tree. This is V10 from a sit start on stacked pads.

❏ **49. Pit Stop Mantel V9** ★ Mantel the small knob at 6 1/2 ft.

❏ **50. Unnamed V3** ★★ Reach high holds and climb straight up.

❏ **51. Bard Mantel V4** ★ Use a gaston crimp to mantel into the scoop.

❏ **52. The Missing Link V4** ★ Start from opposing crimps and climb straight up.

❏ **53. Unnamed V0** ★ Traverse the lip right to the finish of Ament Arête.

❏ **54. Ament Arête V6** ★★ Climb the left angling arête from a sit start. (V4 from a stand start).

❏ **55. Unnamed V0** ★ Climb the face just left of where the two boulders meet.

❏ **56. Unnamed VB** ★ Climb the left arête.

❏ **57. Kauk Slab V8** ★ Climb the slab left of the crack from a stand start. No running.

❏ **58. Unnamed VB** ★ Climb the short crack.

❏ **59. Unnamed VB** ★ Climb the left crack.

❏ **60. Unnamed VB** ★★ Climb the right-angling crack.

❏ **61. Hug a Rock V0** ★★ Start standing with opposing holds and climb straight up.

❏ **62. Torque Spanner V8** ★★ Start in the crack below the roof. Climb out left to the slopey lip. Climb right to the point of the boulder and then mantel.

❏ **63. Anvil Mantel V0+** ★ Mantel the point.

❏ **64. Chapman Overhang V1** ★★ Start on the boulder below the roof and climb out the corner to a jug and mantel. (Var: traverse left at the lip to finish on Anvil Mantel).

Camp 4 - West

Approach time: **3 minutes**

Number of problems: **88**

This sector lies above the west end of the campground. The Wine Boulder is the big boulder directly uphill from the Big Columbia Boulder (with Midnight Lightning).

Titanic Boulder

To find this boulder, continue west on the horse trail past the Pratt Boulder. When the trail turns left to head towards the road, you will see a boulder slightly to the right (if you are facing El Capitan) about 200 ft. away. This is the Titanic Boulder.

❏ **1. Unnamed V3** ★ Start sitting with low crimps and the tree at your back. Climb up and left to mantel.

❏ **2. The Bulge Traverse V7** ★★ Start on #1 and traverse right to #4 finish.

Randy Puro on 6 Degrees (V10).
Photo by Tim Medina.

❏ **3. Unnamed V3** ★ Climb the line just right of the tree from a start with head-height holds.

❏ **4. Battle of the Bulge V6** ★★★ Start on the juggy rail just left of the big jug on the right side. Climb up and left to slopers and then back right to the top out.

❏ **5. The Titanic V5** ★★ Start on the jug at the right side of the rail. Climb straight up past a sidepull crimp.

Number of problems by difficulty

VB	V0	V1	V2	V3	V4	V5	V6	V7	V8	V9	V10	≥V11
16	9	9	9	8	3	9	9	5	3	1	2	4

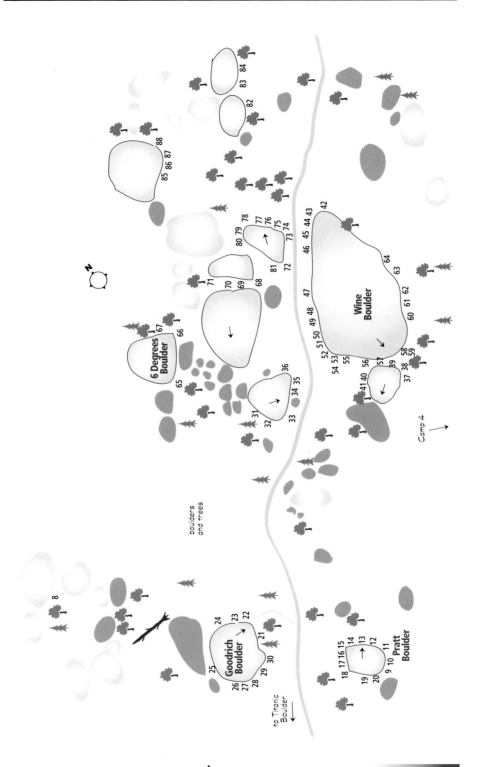

*The next two problems are
on the boulder that is next to
the Titanic Boulder.*

❏ **6. Unnamed V1** ★ Mantel
high edges on the face that
faces Camp 4.

❏ **7. Unnamed V3** ★ Climb
the prow that faces uphill.
Start standing (low start
project).

❏ **8. Unnamed V9** ★★ Start
with a head-height left hand
sidepull. Jump to a right
hand gaston and continue
up and right.

Pratt Boulder

❏ **9. Unnamed V2** ★ Climb
the arête.

❏ **10. The Elegant Gypsy V7** ★★ ! Climb the
left center of the face.

❏ **11. Unnamed V3** ★★ Climb the arête.
Move right and up after a few moves.

❏ **12. Armadillo V3** ★ Climb the pin-scarred
crack.

❏ **13. Unnamed VB** ★★ Jump start to the
flake and climb straight up.

❏ **14. Unnamed V1** ★ Start on a crimpy flake
and climb straight up.

❏ **15. Unnamed V3** ★★ Climb the left arête.
The flake at the bottom is on.

❏ **16. Unnamed V2** ★★ Start on high holds
in the middle of the face. Climb up and left.

❏ **17. Unnamed V2** ★ Start on #16. Go up
and slightly right.

❏ **18. Unnamed V4** ★ Climb the left side of
the arête using edges on the face.

❏ **19. Pablo's Piccola V6** ★ Start on high
small crimps. Go left to an undercling and
then straight up.

❏ **20. Unnamed VB** ★★ Climb the face
directly above the left side of the shelf at the
base.

Goodrich Boulder

❏ **21. Unnamed VB** ★★ ! Start with the right-
facing feature and climb straight up the slab.

❏ **22. Tendons Give V4** ★★★ Sit start the
arête. Traverse right around the corner to a
top out above angled rails.

❏ **23. Tendons Thaw V7** ★★ Climb Tendons
Give and then keep traversing the sloping lip
to a mantel by the tree limb.

❏ **24. Tendons Mend V0** ★★★ ! Start on the
head-height jug in the middle of Tendons
Give. Climb right and up.

❏ **25. Unnamed V6** ★★ Start at the right
side of the lip. Traverse left to the finish of
Tendons Give.

❏ **26. Unnamed V0** ★ Climb the face just
right of the block at the base. Start high.

❏ **27. Unnamed V1** ★ Start on #26 and go right to mantel.

❏ **28. Unnamed V3** ★ Jump to a sloper at the point of the boulder and then mantel.

❏ **29. Unnamed V2** ★ Grab jugs above the flat stone and then climb straight up.

❏ **30. Pinch Arête V3** ★★ Start on chest-height slopers. Go left on arête.

❏ **31. Unnamed VB** ★★ Climb the scooped runnel.

❏ **32. Unnamed VB** ★ Climb the face left of the arête.

❏ **33. Unnamed V5** ★ Climb the arête from a jug sit start.

❏ **34. U.F.O. V7** ! Climb the slab above the rock. (Var: Cash 'em Up V3 climb the slab above the ramp).

❏ **35. Initial Friction V1** ★★ ! Climb the slab left of the arête.

❏ **36. Cocaine Corner V5** ★★★ ! Climb the right side of the angling arête.

❏ **37. Robbins Lieback V1** ★ Start off the cheater stone and climb the left-angling feature.

❏ **38. Unnamed V1** ★ Climb the rounded arête.

❏ **39. Unnamed VB** ★★ Climb the face starting on a good edge at 6 ft.

❏ **40. Marco's Traverse V1** ★ Start on #41 and traverse left to a mantel above edges.

❏ **41. Unnamed VB** ★★ Climb the jugs from a high start.

Sasha Musso on Initial Friction (V1).
Photo by Matt Wilder.

Wine Boulder

❑ **42. Hit Man V5** ★ Start on a high undercling and climb straight up. Top out to the right.

❑ **43. Unnamed VB** ★ Mantel into the scoop at the arête. Then climb up and right.

❑ **44. Unnamed VB** ★ Reach a high angled edge 4 ft. right of the arête and climb straight up.

❑ **45. Unnamed VB** ★★ Stand on stones to reach a flat jug at 7 ft. Climb up, then left, then right.

❑ **46. Unnamed V0** ★ Start on a left-facing flake. Climb up and then go left to finish on #45.

❑ **47. Stick It V11** ★★ Start with a high left hand sloper. Jump to a right hand sloper and continue straight up.

❑ **48. Dominator V12** ★★★★ Start with a left hand edge and a right hand sloper. Climb straight out the roof.

❑ **49. Dominated V13** ★★★★ Sit start the Dominator from an obvious rounded crimp rail.

❑ **50. Fatty Fish V8** ★★ Start with your right hand on the The Phonebook. Jump to a left hand crimp and then traverse left to the finish of Dominator.

❑ **51. The Phonebook V8** ★ Reach the high sloper left of the scoop. Climb right and up.

❑ **52. Unnamed V6** ★ Start palming the left hand sloper in the scoop. Climb straight up.

❑ **53. Unnamed V0** ★★ Climb the arête from a natural cheater stone.

❑ **54. Unnamed VB** ★★ Start on #53 and traverse right along the face to a ramp finish.

❑ **55. Leo's Problem V7** ★ Hand traverse the low sloping rail starting just right of the lowest part.

❑ **56. Millis Mantel V2** ★ Reach high to the protruding sloper and mantel.

❑ **57. Unnamed VB** ★★ Reach to a white jug between the two boulders and traverse left.

❑ **58. The Donini Problem V0+** ★★ ! Jump start to jug and then climb the left side of the arête.

❏ **59. Unnamed** V6 ★ Climb the right side of the arête.

❏ **60. Tap Dance** V10 ★★ Start sitting with a low left-facing sidepull. Climb up and right into the main groove.

❏ **61. Unnamed** V5 ★ Start standing with slopers and climb left to the finish of the Donini Problem.

❏ **62. Wine South Face** V0 ★★★ ! Start high on an angled edge. Climb up, left, and then back right and up.

❏ **63. Lloyd's One Arm Movie Mantel** V0- ★ Mantel the left side of the shelf and then jump down.

❏ **64. Wine Traverse** VB ★★ ! Mantel the jug and then go left to finish on #62.

6 Degrees Boulder

❏ **65. 6 Degrees** V10 ★★ Start on a head-height sloper on the arête. Climb up to a left-facing shallow corner and then pull over.

❏ **66. Team America** V5 ★★ ! Start low near the tree and climb leftwards to the lip. Mantel where the lip turns horizontal.

❏ **67. Baby Bear** V3 ★ Start low with a left-facing hold. Climb straight up.

❏ **68. Robbins Crack** VB ★★ ! Climb the offwidth facing the Wine Boulder that is formed by two boulders.

❏ **69. The Other Side** VB ★ ! Climb the Chimney formed by the two boulders.

❏ **70. Pinball Wizard** V6 ★★★ ! Start on opposing sidepulls. Climb slightly left and then back right and up.

❏ **71. Hammerhead** V5 ★★★ ! Climb the right side of the arête.

Blue Suede Shoes Boulder

❑ **72. E.F. Traverse V3 ★★ !**
Traverse the angled arête.

❑ **73. Indian Rockers V7 ★★** Start
on #74 and continue left along the
lip to join the finish of #72.

❑ **74. Ver's Werner V2 ★★ !** Sit
start the arête.

❑ **75. Red Suede Shoes V5 ★★ !**
Climb the left side of the slab.
(Var: Infrared V5 climb just left of
Red Suede Shoes).

❑ **76. Blue Suede Shoes V5 ★★**
! Climb the slab just left of the
descent. (Var: Purple Suede Shoes
finish on Red Suede Shoes).

❑ **77. Unnamed VB ★★★ !** Climb the
featured right side of the face.

❑ **78. Duck Hit V0 ★★ !** Climb the left arête
of the back face.

❑ **79. Unnamed V1 ★ !** Climb the right arête
of the back face.

❑ **80. Duck Hit Traverse V1 ★★ !** Go up #79
and down #78.

❑ **81. Jenevein Traverse V8 ★** Start by the
trail and traverse the lip left to finish on #79.

❑ **82. Unnamed V0+ ★★** Climb the face from
a high start.

❑ **83. Unnamed V3 ★★** Climb the arête.

❑ **84. Unnamed V0+ ★** Climb the face.

❑ **85. Twinkle Toes V11 ★ !** Start on Rapid
Fire. Go up a few moves and then traverse
left to the blank face. (This has maybe never
been bouldered, only done on TR).

❑ **86. Rapid Fire V6 ★★ !** Climb the flake to
the right-facing feature.

❑ **87. Yo Ho Man V4 ★★ !** Climb the slab just
left of the arête.

❑ **88. Shiver Me Timbers V6 ★★★ !** Start on
high jugs. Climb left to the arête and then
up.

Lyn Verinsky on Pinball Wizard (V6). Photo by Tim Medina.

The Crystals

Approach time: **5-10 minutes**

Number of problems: **14**

This area offers a few more fun problems that are easily accessible from Camp 4. The Crystal problems are classic, but are often covered in moss. Pride is a cool vertical dyno with tiny holds.

Approach

Walk to the west end of Camp 4. Follow the trail that leads west from the south side of the Search and Rescue area. After about 500 ft., this trail comes close to the road and then curves back right. The boulders are shortly after the curve. There is also a small dirt pullout on the road next to these boulders. This pullout is on the right 0.3 miles past the Camp 4 parking lot.

❏ **1. Unnamed V0** ★ Start sitting with a big jug. Climb slightly right and up.

❏ **2. Unnamed V0** ★ Stand start with the big angled undercling. Go up to the lip and mantel.

❏ **3. Project** Climb the prow from a sit start.

❏ **4. Unnamed V0** ★ Traverse the lip from a sit start at the right side.

The Castle

This boulder is often surrounded by water in the spring.

❏ **5. Crystal V2** ★★ Sit start with a right hand juggy crystal hold. Follow the lip left to a mantel at jugs. This is sometimes mossy.

❏ **6. Crystal Direct V3** ★ Start on Crystal and climb straight up.

Scott Chandler on Pride (V9). Photo by Matt Keebler.

Number of problems by difficulty

VB	V0	V1	V2	V3	V4	V5	V6	V7	V8	V9	V10	≥V11
1	5	1	1	3	2	0	0	0	0	1	0	0

❏ **7. Crystal Right** V3 ★ Start on Crystal and climb rightwards to and over a bulging protrusion.

❏ **8. Unnamed** V4 ★ Stand start with crimps above the scoop. Go straight up.

❏ **9. Project** Climb the slopey shelves.

❏ **10. Unnamed** V0 ★★ Hand traverse the lip from left to right.

❏ **11. Unnamed** VB ★ Sit start at good flakes and climb straight up.

❏ **12. Unnamed** V0 ★ Climb the faint dihedral from a high start.

❏ **13. Unnamed** V4 ★ Climb the point of the boulder.

❏ **14. Unnamed** V1 ★★ Climb the rounded left arête.

❏ **15. Pride** V9 ★★★ Start 3 ft. right of the tree. Climb up onto the angled sloping ramp and dyno for the top.

❏ **16. Tree Snake Stap-on** V3 ★★ ! Climb the right arête just left of the little tree. Finish left at the point of the boulder. Boulder A.

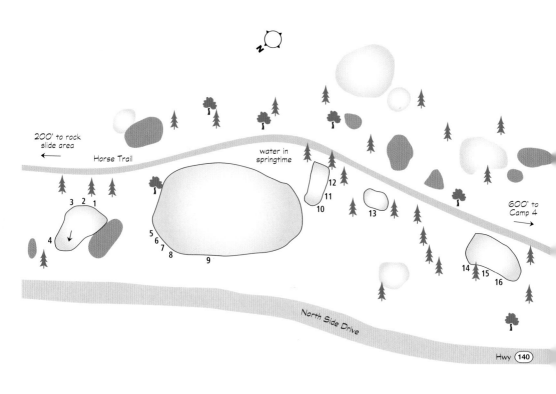

Yabo Boulder

Approach time: **2 minutes**

Number of problems: **1**

This lone boulder, located between Camp 4 and El Capitan, is home to at least three cool problems. The Yabo Roof (a.k.a. Tommy's Roof) is a stunning problem. They say this was a favorite hang of the legendary Yabo.

Approach

There are two dirt pullouts close to each other on the left side 2.0 miles past the Camp 4 parking lot. These are the first two pullouts after the Manure Pile picnic area. Park in the second of these pullouts. You can see the big boulder on the right through the trees just before this pullout. It is right next to the trail.

Tommy Caldwell on Yabo Roof (V11).
Photo by Matt Wilder.

❏ **1. Yabo Face** V11 ★★★ Climb the shallow dihedral on the west side of the boulder just right of a tree.

❏ **2. Yabo Arête** ★★ ! Climb the right arête of the face that is next to the trail. Start from a high jug on the right side.

❏ **3. Yabo Roof** V11 ★★★★ !
(a.k.a. **Tommy's Roof**) Start under the roof with a high undercling. Make long moves out the roof and up the face.

The Bachar Boulder (a.k.a. The El Cap Boulder)

Approach time: **1 minutes**

Number of problems: **3**

This is a cool boulder with a great view of the east face of El Cap. The rock is more featured than typical Yosemite granite and as a result yields some interesting moves.

Approach

Park at the big dirt pullout on the right just before the road curves left to El Cap meadow. This is 2.5 miles past the Camp 4 parking lot. From the parking lot follow a trail towards The Nose of El Cap and a trail sign. After the trail sign, follow another trail to the right and the boulder will be on your right after about 80 ft.

❏ **1. Zodiac V10** ★★ Start on high angled crimps. Climb up and right.

❏ **2. Unnamed V7** ★★ ! Start on an undercling and a sidepull with a tree at your back. Climb up and left and then back right.

❏ **3. Spock Was Here V6** ★★ ! Start right of the tree with a left hand edge and a right hand undercling. Climb up and then go right to a high finish. V8 variation: start on the arete to the right

❏ **4. Silver Tooth of the South V8** ★★★ ! Climb the shallow corner from a jug start.

Josh Williams sending Good Vibrations (V10). Photo by Matt Wilder.

Wood Yard

Approach time: **3 minutes**

Number of problems: **23**

This is another small area that is home to a few classics. The highlight of this area is definitely the MSG Boulder which has a condensed collection of fun climbs. This area is divided into two sections with two different parking areas.

Wood Yard East Approach

Park in a big dirt pullout on the right side of the road 0.7 miles past El Cap Bridge. A dirt road leads up from this pullout.

❏ **1. Steal Your Face V4** ★★ Start at the left arête with a pointy shelf. Climb up and right to holds above the seam.

❏ **2. Unnamed V3** ★ Start on a sidepull and a high crimp. Climb up through angled holds.

❏ **3. Unnamed V3** ★ Climb the arête just right of the moss from a stand start.

Scott Chandler climbing Rudolf Was Adopted (V5).
Photo by Matt Keebler

❏ **4. The End V4** ★★ Start on a curved edge at 4 ft. Go up and right .

❏ **5. Unnamed V0** ★★ ! Climb the face starting from a high pointed jug.

❏ **6. Unnamed V2** ★★ ! Climb #5 from a sit start.

❏ **7. Project** Climb the tufa-like features.

❏ **8. The Wood Yard Arête V6** ★★★ ! Climb the arête right of the tree. Finish slightly right.

❏ **9. Project** Climb the arête.

Number of problems by difficulty

VB	V0	V1	V2	V3	V4	V5	V6	V7	V8	V9	V10	≥V11
2	2	4	2	4	5	1	1	2	0	0	0	0

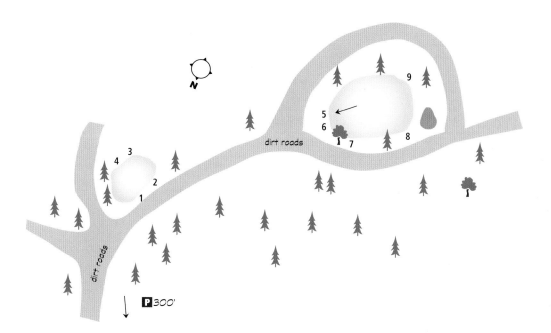

dirt roads

dirt roads

N

P 300'

Wood Yard West Approach

Park in a pullout on the left 0.9 miles past El Cap Bridge. This is just before a paved pullout on the left that has a good view of Bridalveil Falls. You can see the MSG Boulder from the road.

MSG Boulder

❏ **1. Rock Bottom V4 ★★** Traverse the whole boulder in either direction. Start in the center of the face away from the road.

❏ **2. Built to Destroy V4 ★★** Climb the seam in the center of the back face from a sit start.

❏ **3. DSG V2 ★** ! Climb the left side of the arête.

❏ **4. MSG V6 ★★★** ! Climb the right side of the arête.

❏ **5. Rudolf Was Adopted V5 ★★** ! Start on a chest-high curved edge and climb up and right through the center of the face.

❏ **6. U.F.O. II V7 ★★** ! Climb the face below a mossy patch.

❏ **7. Love to Love V1 ★** ! Climb the right arête.

❏ **8. On the Street V3 ★★** Climb straight up from a quartz band shelf.

❏ **9. Unnamed VB ★** Climb the right side of the arête.

❏ **10. Unnamed VB ★** Climb the face.

❏ **11. Lights Out V1** Climb the arête from a shelf start.

❏ **12. Doctor, Doctor V3 ★★** Sit start at the start to Rock Bottom. Climb left and up along the angled crimp rail.

❏ **13. Unnamed V0 ★** Climb the scoop right of the tree. Start on a big sloper.

❏ **14. Blood Groove V1** Climb the mossy slab.

❏ **15. Attack of the Mad Axe Man V1 ★** ! Climb the corner to the mossy slab.

❏ **16. The Victim V4 ★★** ! Climb the sharp arête from a stand start.

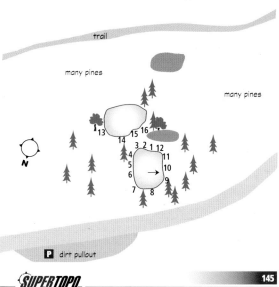

Noah Kaufman on Atlantis (V6). Photo by Matt Wilder.

The Wave

Approach time: **3 minutes**

Number of problems: **19**

This newer area sports a few fun problems. Located downstream from El Cap, this area has a different feel from the center of the Valley. There are more boulders beyond the scope of what is presented here.

Approach

Park in a dirt pullout on the left (south) side of North Side Drive 1.5 miles after its intersection with El Cap Bridge road. You can see the Wave Boulder from the parking.

❏ **1. Unnamed V1** ★ ! Climb the center of the iron colored face / slab.

❏ **2. Sydnie V10** ★★ ! Start standing with edges. Climb straight up to the groove and slopers. This has maybe only been toproped.

❏ **3. Sydnie Arête V1** ★★ ! Climb the right side of the arête from a stand start.

❏ **4. Unnamed V4** ★★ Start sitting on the left side and climb up and right.

❏ **5. Unnamed V3** ★ Climb the arête from a start with a low jug.

The Wave Boulder

❏ **6. The Wave V3** ★★ Climb the arête from a stand start.

❏ **7. Sean Myles Traverse V9** ★★ Start on the right side of the wave feature and traverse left staying fairly low. Finish on The Wave.

❏ **8. Right Side Wave V1** ★ Climb the right side of the wave feature.

❏ **9. Unnamed V2** ★ Climb the face just right of the arête.

❏ **10. Unnamed V2** ★ Climb up through the left-facing edges.

❏ **11. Unnamed V0** ★★ Start high with crimps and climb straight up.

The Generation Boulder

❏ **12. Our Generation V7** ★★★ ! Start on an incut crimper at 5 ft. and climb straight up the face. Finish through edges left of the arête.

❏ **13. Generation Direct V7** ★★ ! Start on Our Generation and climb right to the arête at the halfway point.

Number of problems by difficulty

VB	V0	V1	V2	V3	V4	V5	V6	V7	V8	V9	V10	≥V11
0	1	4	2	4	3	0	0	2	1	1	1	0

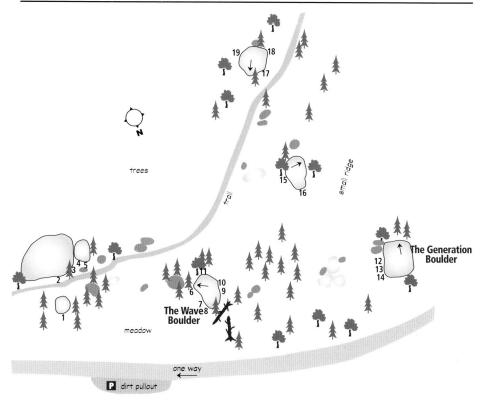

14. My Generation V8 ★★ ! Climb the left side of the arête from a stand start.

15. The Horrification of Laura V3 ★ Start high and climb the seam with edges.

16. Unnamed V4 ★ Start standing with the angled sloper. Go left to the arête and then straight up.

17. Momentum Mantel V3 ★★ Start on high holds left of the small tree. Climb the arête.

18. YI Girl V4 ★★ Start standing at the arête right of the tree. Traverse left on the ledges that lead to a finish on Momentum Mantel.

19. What Girl V1 ★ Start with a shoulder-height jug and climb straight up.

Intersection Boulders

Approach time: **1 minute**

Number of problems: **3**

This fledgling area has lots of potential. In the spring and summer, the boulders by the river may not be climbable.

Approach

When heading out of the Valley, follow Highway 140 left at the 140/120 intersection. Park on the right in a small paved pullout just west of the intersection. There are boulders by the river, boulders between the two roads, and boulders above Highway 120.

The following problems are on the boulder next to the river just down from the parking lot. They face the road.

❏ **1. Atlantis V6** ★★★ Climb the face from a stand start.

❏ **2. Good Vibrations V10** ★★★ Climb the right arête from a sit start. This problem is very height dependent – if you are 6' 4" it may feel like V8, if you are 5' 8" it will probably feel like V11.

The following problem is on the right side of Highway 140 0.6 miles west of the 140/120 intersection.

❏ **3. Heart of Darkness V9** ★★★★ ! Start on a good jug near the left side of the east face and climb straight up on crimps.

Knobby Wall

Approach time: **1 minute**

Number of problems: **2**

This area is not very developed but contains two classics described here. There is potential for more problems here some of which would be suitable for warming up.

Approach

This area is located on the right (south) side of 140 2.0 miles past the intersection of 140 and 120. Park in a paved pullout on the right side of the road. This is the second paved pullout west of Cascade Bridge (the first pullout is just after the bridge). The problems face the road and are located straight back from the west side of the pullout.

❏ **1. Across the Tracks V10** ★★★ Start under the steep face with an angled jug. Go right to a sloper and then up and left to better holds. Finish slightly left.

❏ **2. The Outsider V7** ★★ ! This is on the boulder right of the steep face. Sit start with a jug and the arête. Climb straight up the arête to a slabby finish.

Paul Barraza on Across the Tracks (V10). Photo by Lyn Verinsky.

MORE FROM SUPERTOPO

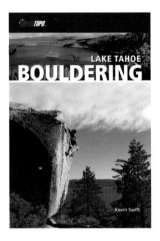

Lake Tahoe Bouldering
Price: $29.95 Available at www.supertopo.com

Lake Tahoe is quickly becoming California's largest summer bouldering area. There are more than 35 areas with more than 1,400 problems and new challenges are discovered every week. What sets Tahoe apart is not just the numbers, it is the variety. You can climb Joshua Tree style rock by the lake or climb Yosemite-esque holds in the forest or drive 30 minutes east to the desert and climb impeccable volcanic pockets. It is all here, it is all year round, and even this book, offering the most complete coverage yet on the subject, can only whet your appetite.

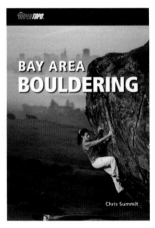

BAY AREA BOULDERING
Price: $24.95 Available at www.supertopo.com

The rock of the Bay Area is as diverse as the landscape and people who live here. Sandstone, schist, rhyolite, basalt and chert are the most prevalent types of stone found locally and they each offer a very unique experience. A few crags with sport and trad climbing can be found around the Bay but the abundance of rock is just the right size for bouldering. This book contains over 600 boulder problems. Many of which have never been published before.

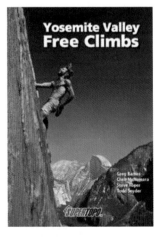

YOSEMITE VALLEY FREE CLIMBS
Price: $29.95 Available at www.supertopo.com

This guidebook includes over 230 of the best routes in Yosemite Valley, from 16-pitch trad climbs to one-pitch sport routes. While many hard Yosemite test-pieces are included, this book focuses on topropes, crags, and multi-pitch climbs in the 5.4-5.9 range. We also include formerly obscure climbs to provide more options for avoiding crowds. As in all SuperTopo books, the authors personally climbed and documented each route with meticulous care to create the most detailed and accurate topos ever published.

MORE FROM SUPERTOPO

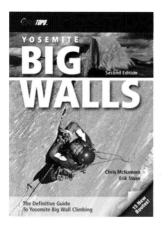

YOSEMITE BIG WALLS - 2nd Ed.
Price: $29.95 Available at www.supertopo.com

Written by Chris McNamara, who personally climbed and painstakingly documented every route, this book includes essential route details such as climbing strategy, retreat information, descent topos, pitch lengths, and gear recommendations for each pitch. Yosemite Big Walls covers the 41 best big wall routes on El Capitan, Half Dome, Washington Column, and Leaning Tower.

TUOLUMNE FREE CLIMBS
Price: $24.95 Available at www.supertopo.com

Tuolumne Free Climbs includes over 110 of the best routes in Tuolumne Meadows, from 14-pitch trad climbs to one-pitch sport routes. This book focuses on topropes, crags, and multi-pitch climbs in the 5.4-5.9 range. Includes formerly obscure climbs to provide more options for avoiding crowds. As in all SuperTopo books, the authors personally climbed and documented each climb with meticulous care to create the most detailed and accurate topos ever published.

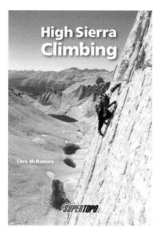

HIGH SIERRA CLIMBING
Price: $24.95 Available at www.supertopo.com

This guidebook includes 26 of the best High Sierra alpine climbs, ranging in difficulty from 3rd class to 5.11c. Most of these climbs are well-protected, 10 to 15 pitches long, and ascend some of the best alpine granite anywhere. Whether you plan to scramble up the 3rd class East Ridge of Mt. Russell, climb the 5.7 East Face of Mt. Whitney, or ascend the epic 18-pitch Sun Ribbon Arête, our guidebook will ensure you spend minimum time getting off-route and maximum time enjoying the climbing.

About the Author:

Matt Wilder has been climbing seriously for the past 13 years. During this time he has climbed and bouldered extensively thoughout the States and Europe. A New England native, he has spent over a month each year in Yosemite for the past 10 years. In addition to bouldering, Matt has a passion for trad and big wall free climbing and has spent many days monkeying around on the Yosemite walls. In the past Matt has worked as a Yosemite pizza shop janitor, a telemarketer, a programming intern, a Rubik's Cube street performer, a guidebook author, a high school math teacher, and a computer science research assistant. He lives in Boulder, CO where he is pursuing a graduate degree in artificial intelligence and computational neuroscience.

Photo by Noah Kaufman

Other Books by Matt Wilder:

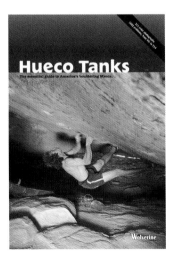

AMERICA'S BOULDERING MECCA
Hueco Tanks

List Price: $32.95 Available at www.wolverinepublishing.com

The essential guide to America's bouldering Mecca. Written by TPWD certified Hueco guide Matt Wilder, who has spent the last seven winters researching the book, it covers all of the bouldering in the entire Park (North Mountain, East Mountain, East Spur, and West Mountain), documenting almost 1700 problems from V0- to V14. The book has sections covering the geology, wildlife, natural, cultural and climbing history of Hueco Tanks, inspirational essays by Fred Nicole, John Sherman, Todd Skinner, Liv Sansoz, and Scott Milton, and all the Beta on Hueco's new rules and regulations. Printed in color, it features over 300 photographs showcasing almost every area in the park. 288 pages, color, sewn binding

Problems Ordered by Grade

- Hard Headed Arête ★★ 44
- Initial Friction ★★ 131
- Lights Out 145
- Love to Love ★ 145
- Marco's Traverse ★ 131
- Mellow Yellow ★ 96
- Pitter-Patter Traverse ★ 108
- Right Mini-Mini ★★ 86
- Right Side Wave ★ 146
- Robbins Lieback ★ 131
- Serendipity 46
- South Arête ★ 64
- Sydnie Arête ★★ 146
- The Glass Pyramid Face ★★ 116
- The Linen Line ★★★ 76
- The Sleeper 124
- Unnamed #2 ★★ 76
- Unnamed #2 ★★ 78
- Unnamed #5 ★★ 53
- Unnamed #5 ★★ 70
- Unnamed #6 ★★ 68
- Unnamed #8 ★★ 116
- Unnamed #9 ★★ 78
- Unnamed #12 ★★ 122
- Unnamed #19 ★★ 118
- Unnamed #20 ★★ 124
- Unnamed #44 ★★ 126
- What Girl ★ 147

V2

- 5150 ★★ 106
- Across the Abyss ★ 90
- Alobar ★ 56
- Birk Crack 96
- Circuit Breaker ★★★★ 78
- Crystal ★★ 136
- Double Decker ★★★ 102
- DSG ★ 145
- Falk's Fracture ★★ 104
- Men From Mars ★ 90
- Millis Mantel ★ 132
- Miss Laid ★ 50
- On The Return ★ 89
- Pump'n Live ★ 96
- Shaggy ★ 45
- Shuttle Face ★★ 72
- The Sloth Left ★ 110
- Unnamed #3 ★★ 68

- Unnamed #4 ★★ 78
- Unnamed #6 ★★ 142
- Unnamed #11 ★★ 78
- Unnamed #11 ★★ 88
- Unnamed #13 ★★ 106
- Unnamed #16 ★★ 130
- Unnamed #17 ★★ 106
- Unnamed #20 ★★ 106
- Unnamed #24 ★★ 80
- Unnamed #29 ★★ 75
- Unnamed #32 ★★ 58
- Ver' Werner ★★ 134
- Wreaker ★ 48
- Yeah! Sit ★★ 46

V3

- A Land Far Away ★★★ 56
- Armadillo ★★ 130
- Baby Bear ★ 133
- Bard's Flying Travers Mantel ★ 122
- California Edge ★ 110
- Cranium Crusher ★★ 74
- Crystal Direct ★ 136
- Crystal Right ★ 138
- Doctor, Doctor ★★ 145
- Door Knocker Traverse ★ 65
- E.F. Traverse ★★ 134
- Get It Up ★★★ 48
- Glass House ★★ 124
- Growing Stone ★ 89
- Hamburger Helper ★★ 88
- Herb ★ 45
- Higgins Problem ★★ 123
- I'm Pumped ★★ 110
- Jonesin' ★★ 48
- Jug of Whine ★★ 100
- Jump Head ★ 124
- Kor Problem ★★ 118
- K-Y Problem ★ 45
- Little Mouse ★★ 37
- Lyn's Awesome Arête ★ 124
- Midget Traverse ★★ 65
- Mini-Stein-Way ★★ 104
- Momentum Mantel ★★ 147
- No Fur ★★ 92
- Oak Leaf Arête ★ 126
- On the Street ★★ 145
- Once Upon a Time ★★★★ 54

- Pinch Arête ★★ 131
- Ray D'Arcy Memorial Problem ★ 45
- Spanish Flies ★ 122
- Stacked ★ 96
- Syndrome ★ 90
- The Angler ★★★ 78
- The Big Moe ★★ 75
- The Horrification of Laura ★ 147
- The James Memorial Problem ★★★ 58
- The Lone Ranger 66
- The Rebirthing ★ 119
- The Robbins Problem ★★ 114
- The Scalpel ★ 100
- The Shrink ★★ 116
- The Sloth ★ 110
- The Wave ★★ 146
- The Zschiesche ★ 116
- Tree Snake Strap-on ★★ 138
- T-rex ★ 89
- Uncle Joe ★★ 124
- Unnamed #1 ★★ 122
- Unnamed #11 ★★ 130
- Unnamed #14 ★★ 89
- Unnamed #15 ★★ 130
- Unnamed #21 ★★ 80
- Unnamed #23 ★★ 106
- Unnamed #32 ★★ 65
- Unnamed #36 ★★ 124
- Unnamed #42 ★★ 126
- Unnamed #43 ★★ 119
- Unnamed #49 ★★ 120
- Unnamed #50 ★★ 81
- Unnamed #50 ★★ 126
- Unnamed #83 ★★ 134
- Unnamed #42 ★★ 58
- Wanna Be ★ 50
- Webb Arête ★★ 124
- What's Next ★★ 44
- Who Knows ★★ 44
- William "The Refrigerator" Perry ★ 95
- Without a Fro ★ 46
- Women From Venus ★ 90

V4

- ❏ Ahwahnee Arête ★★★ 88
- ❏ Amazon Face ★★★ 72
- ❏ Bachar Cracker ★★★★ 118
- ❏ Bard Mantel ★ 126
- ❏ Bear-Hug Mantel ★★ 124
- ❏ Blockead ★★ 123
- ❏ Buckwheat ★★ 76
- ❏ Built to Destroy ★★ 145
- ❏ Cashner-u-al ★ 70
- ❏ Cave Direct ★ 60
- ❏ Crippler ★★ 47
- ❏ Did It Up ★★ 48
- ❏ Feels Like an Oil Slick ★ 47
- ❏ Get It Longer ★ 48
- ❏ Go Go Gorilla ★★ 96
- ❏ Guerneys Gone Wild ★★ 70
- ❏ Ketchup Machine ★ 88
- ❏ Knuckle Fucker ★★ 75
- ❏ Mickey Mouse Traverse ★★ 58
- ❏ Naked and Hairy Traverse ★ 37
- ❏ New Delhi Freight Train ★★ 81
- ❏ Norma ★★ 45
- ❏ Reading Backwards ★★ 54
- ❏ Rock Bottom ★★ 145
- ❏ Smear Out 116
- ❏ Spanish Left ★★★ 66
- ❏ Steal Your Face ★★ 142
- ❏ Tendons Give ★★★ 130
- ❏ The Abtrusion ★★ 64
- ❏ The Bates Problem ★★★ 114
- ❏ The End ★★ 142
- ❏ The Guerin Problem ★★★ 122
- ❏ The Millionth Try ★★ 58
- ❏ The Missing Link ★ 126
- ❏ The Victim ★★ 145
- ❏ To Be Someone ★★ 50
- ❏ Training Bra ★ 95
- ❏ Unnamed #4 ★★ 37
- ❏ Unnamed #4 ★★ 146
- ❏ Unnamed #6 ★★ 74
- ❏ Unnamed #10 ★★ 108
- ❏ Unnamed #11 ★★ 95
- ❏ Unnamed #25 ★★ 118
- ❏ Unnamed #33 ★★ 58
- ❏ White Dike ★ 48
- ❏ Woodward Arête ★★ 118
- ❏ Yabo's Knife ★★ 120
- ❏ YI Girl ★★ 147
- ❏ Yo Ho Man ★★ 134
- ❏ Zorro ★★★ 80

V5

- ❏ Atheletes Die Young ★★ 70
- ❏ Atlas ★★ 90
- ❏ Beached Whale ★★ 91
- ❏ Bionic Traverse ★★ 40
- ❏ Blue Suede Shoes ★★ 134
- ❏ Broken Circuit ★★ 78
- ❏ Bugged ★ 122
- ❏ Cedar Crack ★★ 50
- ❏ Cedar Eater ★★★★ 82
- ❏ Chokin' ★ 92
- ❏ Cocaine Corner ★★★ 131
- ❏ Dead Precedence ★★ 96
- ❏ Extreme Marine ★★ 96
- ❏ Final Departure ★★ 56
- ❏ Flame Thrower ★ 118
- ❏ Grand Larceny ★★ 48
- ❏ Hammerhead ★★★ 133
- ❏ Hard Times ★ 126
- ❏ Hit Man ★★ 132
- ❏ Joe's Garage ★★ 80
- ❏ Juice Man ★ 91
- ❏ Kauk's Crank ★ 75
- ❏ Klingon ★★ 118
- ❏ Ladder Detail ★★ 44
- ❏ Mickey Mouse Extension ★★ 58
- ❏ Peyote ★ 46
- ❏ Red Suede Shoes ★★ 134
- ❏ Road Rage ★ 40
- ❏ Rudolf Wad Adopted ★★ 145
- ❏ Sachmo ★★ 124
- ❏ Smile For The Green Dragon ★★ 90
- ❏ Squeeze ★ 91
- ❏ So Good ★★★ 47
- ❏ Sun Salutation ★ 88
- ❏ Swamp Thing ★★ 119
- ❏ Team America ★★ 133
- ❏ The Bogart Traverse ★★ 44
- ❏ The Cathedral Problem ★★ 45
- ❏ The Fridge ★★ 96
- ❏ The Ruff ★ 58
- ❏ The Titanic ★★ 128
- ❏ Triangle Man ★★ 87
- ❏ Unnamed #4 ★★ 52
- ❏ Unnamed #6 ★★ 37
- ❏ Unnamed #8 ★★ 64
- ❏ End of the Day Problem ★★ 114
- ❏ Unnamed #20 ★★ 103
- ❏ Unnamed #33 ★★ 80
- ❏ Unnamed #34 ★★ 66
- ❏ Unnamed #35 ★★ 66
- ❏ Unnamed #46 ★★ 126

V6

- ❏ 2X2 ★ 94
- ❏ Ament Arête ★★ 126
- ❏ Atlantis ★★★ 148
- ❏ Battle of the Bulge ★★★ 128
- ❏ Blonde Ambition ★★ 90
- ❏ Crossroads Moe ★★★ 36
- ❏ Delicate Flower ★★ 118
- ❏ Denominator ★★ 96
- ❏ Happily Ever After ★★★ 54
- ❏ Heart Attack ★★ 70
- ❏ Hungry for More ★ 123
- ❏ Jungle Book ★★ 64
- ❏ Killing Uncle Joe ★ 124
- ❏ Kudra ★★ 56
- ❏ Louis Variation ★ 47
- ❏ MSG ★★★ 145
- ❏ Munchkin Lunge ★ 92
- ❏ Pablo's Piccola ★ 130
- ❏ Pinball Wizard ★★★ 133
- ❏ Pop Top ★★ 106
- ❏ Rapid Fire ★★ 134
- ❏ Sentinel Traverse ★★★ 64
- ❏ Shiver Me Timbers ★★★ 134
- ❏ Silen Spotter ★★ 91
- ❏ Skatement ★ 37
- ❏ Spanish Fly ★★★ 66
- ❏ Spire Traverse ★ 46
- ❏ Spock Was Here ★★ 140
- ❏ Sports Action Direct ★ 91
- ❏ The Diamond Left ★★ 58
- ❏ The Font Problem ★★ 119
- ❏ The Mechanic ★★ 80
- ❏ The Octagon ★★★ 44
- ❏ The Other Crack ★ 53
- ❏ The Slopster ★★ 64
- ❏ The Wood Yard Arête ★★★ 142
- ❏ Unnamed #13 ★★ 78
- ❏ Unnamed #25 ★★ 130

V7

- ❏ Behave ★★ 48
- ❏ Billy in the Well Low ★ 40
- ❏ Do-Bop ★★★ 38
- ❏ Downward Dog ★ 94
- ❏ Fat Man Traverse ★ 44
- ❏ Fat Weasel ★★ 126
- ❏ Fine Line ★★ 72
- ❏ Fish Head ★★ 44
- ❏ Flake Out ★★ 64
- ❏ Full Sail ★★ 45
- ❏ Generation Direct ★★ 146
- ❏ Half Pint ★★ 86
- ❏ Indian Rockers ★★ 134
- ❏ Joss ★ 91
- ❏ Leo's Problem ★ 132
- ❏ No Holds Bard ★★★ 64
- ❏ Our Generation ★★★ 146
- ❏ Prowess ★★★ 72
- ❏ Rubik's Revenge ★★ 95
- ❏ Seat of the Pants ★ 118
- ❏ Silly Roof ★★ 88
- ❏ Spanish Right ★★ 66
- ❏ Sports Action ★ 91
- ❏ Stinkbug ★ 122
- ❏ Tendons Thaw ★★ 130
- ❏ The Bulge Traverse ★★ 128
- ❏ The Elegant Gypsy ★★ 130
- ❏ The Flapping Shoe ★★ 76
- ❏ The Hexcentric ★★★ 44
- ❏ The King ★★★ 48
- ❏ The Outsider ★★ 148
- ❏ Torque ★★★ 72
- ❏ Tweety Bird ★ 94
- ❏ U.F.O. 131
- ❏ U.F.O. II ★★ 145
- ❏ Unnamed #2 ★★ 140
- ❏ Unnamed #8 ★★ 37
- ❏ Unnamed #24 ★★ 89
- ❏ Yosemite Speedway Traverse ★ 40

V8

- ❏ 4x4 ★★ 94
- ❏ All Hands on Deck ★★ 124
- ❏ Big Bird ★ 94
- ❏ Bruce Lee ★★★ 124
- ❏ Clean and Jerk ★ 118
- ❏ Collins Direct 75
- ❏ Deliverance ★★★ 53
- ❏ Fatty Fish ★★ 132
- ❏ Flatline ★★★ 70
- ❏ Front Seat ★★ 89
- ❏ It Seams So ★ 64
- ❏ Jenevein Traverse ★ 134
- ❏ Kauk Face ★★ 85
- ❏ Kauk-a-holic ★ 118
- ❏ King Cobra ★★★★ 118
- ❏ Little Blue Anasthesia ★★ 87
- ❏ Midnight Lightning ★★★★ 114
- ❏ My Generation ★★ 147
- ❏ Myles Traverse ★★ 92
- ❏ Octagon Traverse ★ 44
- ❏ Pommel Horse ★★ 89
- ❏ Purple Barrel ★★ 75
- ❏ Rabbit Habbit ★★ 72
- ❏ Slapshot ★★ 64
- ❏ Sonic Wave ★★ 124
- ❏ The Changing Corners ★★★ 58
- ❏ The Diamond ★★★ 58
- ❏ The First Glasses ★★ 80
- ❏ The Phonebook ★ 132
- ❏ Toe Licker ★★ 45
- ❏ Torque Spanner ★★ 127
- ❏ Silver Tooth of the South ★★★ 140

V9

- ❏ Candy Ass ★★ 124
- ❏ Conan ★★ 70
- ❏ Crazy Horse ★★ 94
- ❏ Crytpchild 89
- ❏ Don't Make Me Kick Your Ass ★★ 114
- ❏ Funky Chicken ★★ 92
- ❏ Heart of Darkness ★★★★ 148
- ❏ Honor Among Thieves ★★★ 119
- ❏ Jitterbug ★★ 56
- ❏ Kauk Start ★ 114
- ❏ Midnight Cowboy ★ 114
- ❏ Montezuma's Revenge★★★ 95
- ❏ Piranha ★★ 72
- ❏ Pit Stop Mantel ★ 126
- ❏ Plastic Surgery ★ 122
- ❏ Pressure Drop ★★ 89
- ❏ Pride ★★★ 138
- ❏ Pugelist ★★ 88
- ❏ Sean Myles Traverse ★★ 146
- ❏ Sex Factor X ★★★ 119
- ❏ The Force ★★★ 120
- ❏ The Misfit ★★ 87
- ❏ Unnamed #8 ★★ 130
- ❏ Unnamed #17 ★★ 86

V10

- ❏ 6 Degrees ★★ 133
- ❏ Across the Tracks ★★★ 148
- ❏ After Midnight ★★ 114
- ❏ Cilley ★ 88
- ❏ Darth Maul ★★ 70
- ❏ Drive On ★★★★ 87
- ❏ Ghost Rider ★★ 87
- ❏ Goldmund ★★★ 72
- ❏ Good Vibrations ★★★ 148
- ❏ Jackie Chan ★★ 124
- ❏ Leroy ★★ 120
- ❏ Sharma Variation ★★ 126
- ❏ Sydnie ★★ 146
- ❏ Tap Dance ★★ 133
- ❏ The Moffat Start ★★★ 114
- ❏ The Wizard ★★ 45
- ❏ Thong Cave ★★ 91
- ❏ Thriller ★★★★ 120
- ❏ X ★★★ 44
- ❏ Zodiac ★★ 140

V11

- ❏ Narcissus ★★★ 72
- ❏ Stick It ★★ 132
- ❏ The Shield ★★ 70
- ❏ Yabo Roof ★★★★ 139
- ❏ Twinkle Toes ★ 134
- ❏ Yabo Face ★★★ 139

V12

- ❏ Chimera ★★ 94
- ❏ Dominator ★★★★ 132
- ❏ Park Life ★★★ 107
- ❏ Scissors for Lefty ★★ 119
- ❏ The Shadow Warrior ★★★★ 58

V13

- ❏ Dominated ★★★★ 132

Index

CLIMBERS, the **ENVIRONMENT** and **ACCESS**
are all interconnected
Know how you fit in. ▸▸

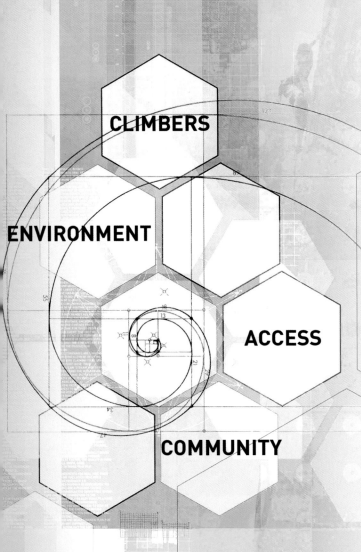

CLIMBERS

ENVIRONMENT

ACCESS

COMMUNITY

LOCAL LOW DOWN
▸▸Someone owns the land that you're climbing on and chances are it's not you. Respect their regulations, including closures.
▸▸Check websites, guidebooks, and talk to locals- not only do they know the best lines, they know the beta to keep the areas open.
▸▸If you're a local be informed and care about what happens at your area.

CLIMB STEALTH
▸▸Keeping nature pristine keeps it...well...natural.
▸▸Off-trail travel accounts for the greatest environmental impacts by climbers - stay on established trails.
▸▸Protect plants from packs, pads, gear sprawl, and feet; stay on durable surfaces - uh, like rocks.
▸▸Stupid Check? Before you leave, look around, pick-up and pack-out tape, spilt chalk, wrappers, cig butts, whiskey bottles...even if they're not yours.

SPEAK UP SPEAK OUT
▸▸When the actions of others threaten access or the environment, let 'em know- sometimes we all need a little tap on the shoulder
▸▸Don't just be a person who climbs, be a **climber** (psst...se everything above).

POWERED BY CLIMBERS
join at www.accessfund.org

ACCESS FUND
your climbing future